I0569357

GOOD TO

GREAT

GRANDPARENTING

A Guide to Lasting Meaningful Connections

Neil Taft

Neil Taft

Good To Great Grandparenting

Copyright © 2024 Neil Taft
All rights reserved.
ISBN: 979-8-9902957-0-4

Neil Taft

Mission Statement

You are a GOOD Grandparent, or you wouldn't be reading this. Our Mission is to foster Greatness through Lasting Meaningful Connections with your Grandchildren by sharing stories, ideas, and resources with the purpose of spurring your own idea machine.

Neil Taft

Table of Contents

INTRODUCTION

> "You have been given a gift. Actually, You are a gift. You are a Grandparent."
>
> Neil Taft

> "Nobody can do for little children what grandparents do. Grandparents sort of sprinkle stardust over the lives of little children."
>
> Alex Haley

You will be a Grandparent for twice as long as you were a parent. You are a much more active and mobile Grandparent than your own Grandparents were. Your Grandchildren will live at a greater distance from you than families in generations past. Your Grandchildren have access to an exponentially greater amount of knowledge at a much younger age than you or your children did. You have a window into their world that never existed for your Grandparents.

I am writing this book to help Grandparents rise to the next level of the experience we call Grandparenting. This level doesn't require any of us to become something we are not; it simply provides a path to become more of who we are and who we want to become. My approach will be to offer each of my readers Food for Thoughtfulness.

Welcome!

As Grandparents, we are at our highest and best selves when we are acting on our gift and doing all we can to be a meaningful influence on and a stable force for our Grandchildren. With the earned wisdom of our years, we will realize that if we just try to let Grandparenting happen as many of our Grandparents did, the outcome may be okay, but I, for one, am not willing to settle for just okay when it comes to all these little miracles that I call my Grandchildren. There are definitely things we can learn from others, understand better, and, if appropriate, act on them to make this Journey worth investing in wholeheartedly. This can best be realized by getting to know each Grandchild at a molecular level and being a positive support for and partner with their parents whenever possible. This is foundational to maximizing our role as Great-Grandparents. The best and sometimes the most challenging task is surrendering ourselves to the reality of the tide of the times. This adventure involves a better understanding of the world that our Grandchildren inhabit and a bit about us evolving beyond parenting the parents of our Grandchildren, hence Good to Great. The word that comes to mind is finesse. Finesse requires attention and intention. As much as we all crave a magic pill to cure all ills, the reality is that we know that doesn't exist. This is especially true when it comes to the inherent messiness of extended families and the complexities of life in general. That doesn't mean we throw up our hands in surrender. I look at it as more of a marathon of thoughtfulness. One step, one person, one circumstance at a time. It is much more like a daily vitamin than a cure-all pill.

> **"The smallest change in perspective can transform a life."**
> **- Oprah Winfrey**

As an illustration, let me tell a story about myself. I believe the statute of limitations has run its course, so they can't come get me for child endangerment now.

Back in the early 1970's, when we embarked on a road trip as a family, it went like this. Upon departure, my copilot/wife fell asleep as I backed out of the driveway. Shortly afterward, my then 3-year-old daughter nodded off in the back seat. That left my son, the chatterbox, and I to drive through the night and keep each other entertained and awake. At the time I was driving a Datsun station wagon with bucket seats in the front. At the age of four or so, my son liked to stand in the gap between the front seats so he could pepper me with a rapid-fire series of unanswerable questions. Before you get all excited with your OMGs, try to remember that this was an entirely different era when it came to children and automobile travel. Bear with me for a moment and I will attempt to redeem myself.

I enjoyed my time and conversations with him, as I still do today, but naturally, I was concerned about his safety. I worked at National Airlines in Miami at the time, so I went to the fabrication shop and asked a friend of mine to sew together a cargo net deal that was strapped between the front seats to protect him in the event I had to suddenly slam on the brakes. This rather rudimentary Rube Goldberg contraption allowed us to continue our "visits" as I drove. It also kept my son occupied, without disturbing the peaceful slumber of either my wife or daughter.

Today's car makers, child safety seat manufacturers, and child protection laws are far more sophisticated and far better monitored than they were at that point in time. Back then there were still many cars on the road that didn't even have driver or passenger seatbelts, much less rear-facing safety seats or laws making it illegal to travel with children under a certain age sitting in the front seat of a vehicle.

My point is that a startling number of things in our world have experienced drastic changes in the 50 years since my own kids were small, but then, so have I. I've learned quite a bit over that period of time, certainly far more than mere vehicle safety standards.

The objective of this book is to share what I've learned about grandparenting, which as it turns out, was a challenge far more daunting than any of us could have ever begun to imagine.

I continued to learn and, in the process, managed to keep track of what works and what doesn't in today's world. Hopefully, what I've learned will help other Grandparents navigate this curious yet still wondrous journey. I would not trade those priceless conversations with my son for the world, but knowing what I know now, for my grandchildren I'd do it differently. Now I consult with the parents before any trip like that with my Grandchildren and follow all the guidelines they gave me.

Tip: Start early to change over to the infant rear-facing car seat, the 1-3 rear-facing car seat, the 4-7 car seat with harness, and the 4-7 booster seat.

The power of parents and Grandparents operating in unison in the best interest of the Grandchild cannot be overstated. This is Familial Love in action. This synergy adds value to the all-important secure attachment that allows children to grow and thrive. It is not an exaggeration to tout the advantage of a unified effort to offer our little Loves the absolute best chances to develop and grow to their own potential bathed in a sense of feeling Loved.

For the best possible outcome in the family setting this may require that the Grandparents reframe the traditional model of Grandparenting. For most, it is not a major shift in thought but rather a reconsideration. A Thoughtfulness mindset.

Depending on where you begin this Journey, you may have to do some soul-searching; for others, it will require a few adjustments. No matter the degree of difficulty, working in partnership with the parents has the greatest return on investment. It is difficult but essential and appropriate to learn, relinquish the reins, add value, and trust your own ability to create a Great outcome. Some of the most evolved, effective, and supportive Grandparents carry around a metaphorical roll of duct tape to put over their mouths to keep themselves from offering unsolicited advice to their children about how to raise *their* kids. This is important enough to repeat; they are *their* kids. To quote the most influential wise person in my life, my Mom always told us, "If you don't have something nice to say don't say anything at all." This may just be the best advice EVER when it comes to backing off and letting our children raise their own children. This cannot be emphasized enough. You did a good job raising them and now it is your turn to stand back and trust them with the process. Given room, encouragement, and support, you may find that they will come to you now and then to ask for advice. Oh, Happy Day, it is now appropriate, standing shoulder to shoulder, side by side, to venture into this delicate territory of advising.

The number one concern among Grandparents is the health and well-being of their Grandchildren. The closer we are with the parents of our Grandkids the better our chances of reaching that goal. This partnership with Mom and Dad creates a synergy that will benefit all, especially your Grandchildren. One of the positive upsides of maintaining an open channel with the parents is that you can glean valuable information about what is happening with your Grandchildren. This information allows you to bond with them over what interests them at any given moment. One of the six principles in Dale Carnegie's best-selling book, "How to Win Friends and Influence People" is to "Speak in terms of others' interests." Ahhh, yes, meaningful connection. Much of what you will read in the coming pages has to do with meeting each Grandchild where they are and being intentional about creating and nurturing a lasting meaningful connection with them. This is kind of the "secret sauce" if you will.

This book is a collection of information, real stories, and experiences that illustrate what has and hasn't worked for many Grandparents with the hope that it may foment ideas of support, understanding, and connection in your own unique relationships with your Grandchildren.

Intentional Grandparenting is paradoxically unique, and yet, as Grandparents, we have many shared desires, challenges, and hopes. In my first Grandparenting book, "NO GREATER LOSS," from back in 2010, I proffered that "Life is complicated, family life is a multiple of complicated, and extended family life is exponentially complicated." Much of this book is about how best to assemble this jigsaw puzzle we call extended family, achieving the best outcome for our precious Grandchildren without falling victim to agendas other than our goal to do the best we can with the reality that exists.

Within each family, there is usually a broad spectrum of circumstances regarding how families function, or not. It is in this family history context that we must dig deep into our own and other Grandparents experience, patience, compassion, and wisdom to invest all we can on behalf of "The best interest of our Grandkids" above the noise and messiness of life in the world and the family. I am reminded of an observation that may apply here. "The road to the gold mine is usually a bumpy dirt road."

Your experience and your relationships with your Grandchildren are just that, they are yours. All of us want to get it as right as we can. We are on this Journey to get it as right as we can. When it comes to your extended family there is your truth and when it comes to my extended family there is my truth. The odds are those will be very different truths. There may even be a great disparity in the understanding of the truth between you and the extended family member you are dealing with. It is incumbent upon us to do the best we can with whatever that reality is. Be intentional in doing the best you can with whatever the circumstances are with your family. It is to that end that I am sharing so many diverse stories and circumstances. Most times, the word *easy* doesn't enter the conversation, but our Grandkids are worth the effort. Tyler Perry's Grandmother offered him a bit of wisdom when it comes to something not being easy; she reminded him that, "If the mountain was flat the view from the top would not be so spectacular."

As Grandparents we are blessed with a unique power within the family. An awesome opportunity to enhance our own lives by elevating the potential and sense of self-worth of our Grandchildren. In today's vernacular that is referred to as our own SuperPower. One mature lady was overheard saying "I am a Grandmother, what is your SuperPower?" This SuperPower can make Unconditional Love of our Grandkids a downhill Journey.

Like all of us, our Grandchildren are reaching for significance. It is our job to give them a boost.

Grandpa NEIL

Chapter 1

YOU ARE HERE / WE ARE HERE

> "The beginning is the most important part of the work."
> Plato

My bride of 30 years (The Grandkids called her Mimi) and I lived close to the massive Southpark Mall in Charlotte, North Carolina. She knew it well, me, not so much. With many entrances when I first walked in, I found one of those "You are Here" kiosks to help me find my way.

In your quest to become the best Grandparent you can be, a good place to start is by creating your own "You are Here" kiosk and if you are a couple, it is wise to also create a "We are Here" kiosk to know where you wish to go from where you are now. The outcome of your journey will be greatly improved if you decide where you are and just where it is that you want to go. As with many things having to do with Grandparenting, there will probably be a marked difference between how a Grandpa approaches this Journey and how a Grandma does it. Both are right, but it is also good to consider how you, as a "We", will approach some of these activities and events. Here you are all dressed up, wearing your finest and most Noble Intention, Loving Care, Wisdom, and Desire. Where do you go from here and what is the most effective way to get there?

As you plan your place and path for this Journey, bear in mind that being a Grandparent offers you an opportunity that is unique to your situation. You have the potential and honorable intention to help each of your Grandchildren feel more Significant and Loved. Just pause and take that in for a moment. This is an awesome and sacred role unique to you. Keep in mind that Lasting Meaningful Connections with your Grandchildren add so much value to that child, it also adds value to you and creates your Legacy. It will be the story they remember and tell others about you.

When I was a youth minister at our church, I used to urge my kids to find and foster a relationship with at least one significant adult other than a parent in their lives. Someone who helps them to feel safe and secure and that they know has their best interest at heart. This may be your chance to apply for that position. I hope you get the job.

A good place to start is to decide where You are, and where you wish to go. It is up to you to be realistic about your circumstances. Many things are relevant to how your journey will play out. Things like the size of your family, Geography, Strength of your relationships with your own children and their spouses, your health, your level of commitment, your finances, etc. Chances are good that you have a smorgasbord of family dynamics, and each situation will require a unique plan. This is your journey, and you get to decide how you take it within the unique circumstances of your family as well as the unique circumstances of your daughter-in-law, or son-in-law's family.

Warning (Marathon in progress!) This is a significant and complex Journey. Each action we take is almost imperceptible. Note I said "almost".

Just as you have a smorgasbord of family dynamics, after reading this book you will also have an even greater smorgasbord of ideas, insights, and ways to make this an exciting and mutually meaningful Journey. In addition, you will come away with some of the most important information about signs signaling trouble ahead. Recognize your feelings of being overwhelmed and put them back in the closet. I have been studying and writing about this stuff for decades and I even get a little overwhelmed at times. Not all these ideas are for everyone. Choose your starting point and begin. Don't fall prey to (my own procrastination favorite) overthinking things to the point of feeling overwhelmed. One wise person expounded that "Perfection is the enemy of done." The antidote to feeling overwhelmed is action. Assess where you are and begin. Just start by sending one thoughtful text. My favorite go-to is, "Just thought of you and it made me smile!" Text is often better than the telephone. Phone calls are often ignored, but kids read every one of their text messages.

Let me share a story of how powerful a text message out of the blue can be. About once a week I send out texts (electronic hugs) to those of my Grandkids who are off at school, etc. Just a simple "You are Supercalifragilisticexpialidocious" or something like that, and I usually get a warm reply. This past weekend I thought of including my first (and now grown) 34-year-old Grandson. It went like this; "While writing my Grandparenting book it brought back fond memories of hanging out with you. Our Helicopter ride, (a first for both of us), along with Monster Trucks and race cars. I think there is a theme of motors here. Hope you are doing well." His reply came swiftly; "Very Well. I'm actually taking Little Dionte (my nephew) to go see some Monster Trucks tomorrow! I'm not sure who is more excited, me or him! (smiley face emoji) I wrote back. "The apple doesn't fall far from the tree" ☺

Here is the amazing payoff for this ole Grandpa.

"I think about those same memories with you all the time too. I was just telling someone yesterday about my first ride in an airplane when we went to Chimney Rock. All those times we went and raced Go-karts. I still have my signed photo of Jeff Gordon that you got me too…and my mom's signed photo of Harry Gant on a motorcycle!! (I'm assuming that one came from you as well) I'm not sure I've ever officially thanked you for all the great times we've had. But genuinely, they meant more than you'll ever know. I didn't have a lot of great memories with anyone as a kid. Pretty much all those came from you. Best of all, I learned from you how to pass that same gift down to other kids and try my best to be that person for every kid I can. So seriously, THANK YOU!!! I love you, Grandpa."

"Love you back."

In baseball that is considered a Grand Slam! This calls for another Oh, Happy Day!

If texting is not your thing you can send a card or letter by snail mail or even a call "For no reason other than wanting to talk with them". You are embarking upon hopefully the most valuable and fun Journey of a Lifetime. Enjoy the ride.

To derive the most from this Journey, your results will depend upon your own vision of who you are and just how Great you would like to be as a Grandparent. The potential for creating more Love and Connection with your Grands is vast and unbounded. I encourage you to take stock of your own values and hopes for your family. We communicate better when we are standing on clear values, boundaries, and realities. The clearer these are to you, the better chance you have to affect the outcome you dream about. In some families it may be more difficult, but your odds are greatly enhanced if you see the possibilities, act on them, and stay the course.

Let's look at those clear Values, Boundaries, and Realities:

Values. Much like passing the baton in a relay race, you will be sharing your own values with your Grandkids. Your core values will be obvious because children closely watch your every move. During my Youth Ministry days, I attended a couple of Self-Esteem seminars being presented by Jack Canfield,

The Chicken Soup for the Soul Guy. One of the things I took away from that was to identify and act upon Core Values. It took a lot of work, but once I zeroed in on my own Core Values, they continued to serve me well, even all these many years later. I keep them top of mind and it has helped me in countless ways. Especially in clearly communicating what I am willing to do and what I am not willing to do, and -------------- what I am not.

An example of this was presented in a podcast that made a lot of sense to me. The speaker stated that when he visited his now remarried daughter's family he operated on the adage of "When in Rome do as the Romans do" On the Sunday mornings they were visiting their kids' family, Grandma and Grandpa went to church where the family attended even though it was a different denomination than theirs. When the Grandkids came to their home, they all attended Grandma and Grandpa's Church.

This simple solution conveyed a strong family unity message to the Grandchildren. The added benefit is that all have their horizons broadened; this solution communicates clear values and prevents conflict. I find this idea to be unifying and brilliant. As a wise man once said, "Why not both/and instead of either/or?"

Thoughtful things like this can go a long way to setting an atmosphere of cooperation.

Boundaries. Having boundaries and clearly communicating with them is one of the fundamental building blocks of a long and mutually beneficial relationship. It helps us all keep it on the road when it comes to doing all that we can but not getting bowled over by someone else's inattention to other's feelings.

I hear countless stories from Grandparents about parents that overuse and sometimes abuse things like babysitting. Some parents just assume that Grandma has nothing better to do. This line gets squishy all too often. Boundaries are the best weapon against insidious forces of resentment.

In some families, more clarity around finances is needed. Other frequent occurrences of pushing boundaries come around how we celebrate holidays as a family. The list can be long, but it is up to you as the Grandparent to decide and then make clear what your boundaries are. Being specific is a great way to bracket your boundaries. Something like; "I am available to babysit every Tuesday and Wednesday evening if that helps you and your husband to get some things done." or, "We won't be able to make it for Thanksgiving this year, but we still would Love to see you. How about earlier in November?"

Most kind and gentle people have trouble with boundaries. Most families don't like to talk about these kinds of things. That is understandable. You don't need to become someone you are not, but it will serve all for you to decide on some boundaries and communicate them to all concerned. This sometimes-tricky area is the source of some resentments that, with time, fester and grow.

My guiding rule is that I try not to get into anything I will resent or regret. This guide helps me to bracket my boundaries.

Realities. This is an extended family and sometimes it is not easy to navigate. One reality that most people just gloss over is whether they are maternal or paternal Grandparents. This is probably the most significant factor of all. Like it or not, there is an implied hierarchy in these extended families, with the Mother of the Grandchildren at the top, and the father next in line. To deny this hierarchy will cause all kinds of Grandparent disappointment.

With the 50% plus divorce rate on first marriages, this is something that will probably touch half of you reading this. The statistics are even worse on second marriages. In one family I read about there are 12 living Grandparents. WOW! Can you imagine Thanksgiving dinner?

If people know the realities, then doors to clear communication are more open. Your approach to extended family life must be done with eyes wide open. It doesn't make it impossible, but it does present a few challenges. Understanding the realities helps to prevent a buildup of petty jealousy and resentment.

Your "Here" is unique, and each of us has different gifts, challenges, abilities, interests, and limitations when it comes to our Grandkids. Each of us also has unique family circumstances and resources that we need to consider honestly and clearly. Each of us brings a unique history to the table. Each of us has our own Hopes and Dreams for our Grandchildren.

It will be valuable to take a moment and think about your own beliefs about things such as Faith, Finances, Health, Education, Discipline, etc. It is equally valuable to **honestly** assess your own as well as the circumstances of each member of your extended family. This is your Journey, and it is incumbent upon you to decide just how Great your commitment is and how best to add the Greatest value to your Grandchildren and, by extension, to your entire family. Armed with this honest assessment it will be easier to form a partnership with their parents to get the best outcome for your Grandchildren.

As I have drilled down into Grandparenting over these past dozen years I have been amazed at two things. The vast majority of Grandparents have an enormous desire to do all they can to help their kids and Grandkids thrive and flourish. The other thing I have come to know is that our unique position as Grandparents has a Power and Dynamic that doesn't show up anywhere else in the family structure or in the universe for that matter. Our task is to strategically apply what we know with what we learn about Grandparenting in the 21st century and to bring these two SuperPowers to bear on our best possible family outcomes.

The learning part of this equation begins with your "You are here/We are here Kiosk." One effective way to do this is to take stock.

Generations X, Y, and Z call them vision boards; I call them Legal Pads. I have simply taken stock of my family, my circumstances, and my vision of how I can be the best Grandparent that I can be, starting from "HERE". Look, by now, if we are awake and aware, we know how complicated families can be, so being honest with yourself and your trusty legal pad will be helpful to know where you are starting from on your journey. Some paths will be downhill, some uphill and possibly some will appear impassable, but that shouldn't dissuade us from exploring each of those paths. As with my Journey on behalf of my Grandchildren, the title of this book is similarly Intentional.

The now famous business book, "Good to Great" by Jim Collins, which was published in 2001, sold over four million copies. I read the book twice a couple of decades ago. Its popularity extended far beyond the traditional business book audience.

One of the nuggets of wisdom I gleaned from the author's book was that he believed the companies he studied and had written about at the time had been Built to Last, in order to have ultimately reached that level of success. Since much of my working career entailed building stuff, this was a concept I understood and could do, and you can do it as well.

Consequently, my contribution to my family is helping to Build Resilience in my Grandchildren so that they can thrive and flourish, then pass it along to future generations. The term Legacy comes to mind, and I want mine to add value to as many people as I can, especially my beloved Grandchildren. How about you?

The process of assessing your "Here" is a lot like the preparation for making out your will. There are a ton of resources to help you. As a Grandparent, AARP is a great source of Articles, lists and resources offered by like-minded folks at similar stages of life. I encourage you to begin.

This process often has the added benefit of reminding us of all the extraordinary things we must be grateful for in our family. For me, Gratitude is the fuel of becoming the Greatest Grandpa I can be!

Here are some of the primer questions I asked myself before I began my Journey. (A more in-depth list of possible questions can be found on the companion website for this book, https://goodtogreatgrandparenting.com in the "You as a Grandparent" category).

When you answer these questions, it is useful to answer from your own perspective but, equally important, how you think each person would answer these same questions about how they see you.

1. How are things with my own children?
2. Their spouses? (Present and past)
3. My Grandchildren.
4. What do you have and what are you willing to invest in terms of time and resources on this Journey?
    Tip: The amount of time, brutal self-honesty, and effort you invest in these questions will be directly proportional to the degree of success you will have on your Journey.
5. What do you need to learn, consider, and do to be the best Grandparent you can be?
6. How do you think each of your Grandchildren rank you as a Grandparent? (I am a 1-10 kind of guy)
7. What do you need to learn about present day methods of communicating with your family? i.e. - The internet, Social Media, etc.

I would like to underline, bold, and italicize the first four for just a moment. What we do is important, but it is equally important to consider how what we do is perceived, especially in the case of extended family interactions. I once read a story that kind of points up this idea succinctly. In his Memoir, "Days of Grace" by; Arthur Ashe, the Tennis Great, recalls some marriage instructions he and his fiancée, Jeanne, received just prior to their wedding. Their minister was then The United States Ambassador to the United

Nations, Andrew Young. The Reverend Young told them about the 6 people he would be marrying the next day. He went on to clarify by explaining, "You see, when you and Jeanne get married tomorrow, six people will be involved. With each of you, there are really three "persons". First, there is the person you are. Next, there is the person you think you are. Then there is the person others think you are.

For this exercise to be most effective and useful to your Journey all three of these aspects of who you are must be considered. I know that is a lot, but people's perceptions are their reality in most cases. I offer this as food for thought, not as an absolute.

I promise you that this evaluation process is as rewarding as it is difficult to complete but that is no excuse for not beginning in earnest. One example of how this happens is illustrated by a couple who have a slew of Grandkids. To keep them all straight they have a loose-leaf binder and each of their Grands has their own page(s) to help the Grandparents remember things like birthdays, upcoming events, present interests, Friends names (especially their Grandchild's Best Friend), accomplishments, school contact information, etc. I include a space for my Hopes and Dreams for each child. More on this in the chapter on Effectiveness. These Hopes and Dreams, aside from being instructive and fun to do, often change as your Grandchild grows.

This is an effective way to evaluate each branch of your extended family as well. Remember these pages are for your eyes only.

So, as you plan out your next step it will be useful to go through this same vision exercise you did for yourself, but for each of your Grandchildren. I have a loose-leaf binder (Mine is titled "The Treasure Trove") with pages of stuff on each Grandchild. Truth time: I admit (I am a sentimental old coot) I still have all their artwork and "I Love You Grandpa" notes adorning the walls of my living room and office, some of which are turning brown and getting dog eared over these past 35 years. This binder helps me and my questionable memory to get the facts straight. This may not be your experience, but my Grandchildren grow up sooooo fast. Each Grandchild has their own page(s).

In my case my youngest Grandchild is 15 so his pages have grown to include things like his college plans, school stuff, girls of course, other new interests, books we both like, academic milestones and/or challenges, and on and on. Their parents are an invaluable source of information as well.

I doubt you can possibly have too much information on each one. My main source of current information is listening to them. Keep in mind that the quality of your questions will determine the quality of the information. When I know, I am going to see them I review our last conversation, and instead of assuming things are the same, I ask for an update on so and so, or some project they were working on. This way they know they are being heard and that I am genuinely interested in the specifics of what is going on for them.

One such conversation was with my then, 15-year-old Granddaughter, and her13-year-oldd brother. We were sitting at the dining room table at their house talking about this and that. The conversation was going well so I ventured out onto the high dive. I set the question up with my usual please help me to understand your world. I asked, "What kind of things scare you"? The answers came fast and furious. We wandered through all kinds of subjects from horseback riding too fast, to snakes, to politics, to bullies, and to disappointing their parents. Somewhere during this time my daughter in-law walked past and sat and joined us. It was amazing. It was almost like one sibling caused the other to add something. It was a most meaningful conversation. I have revisited it with each of them individually. Some of the stuff has changed but none has surpassed that one day. It is amazing what can be accomplished if you simply ask.

To be thorough I also include a regular conversation with their parents about each one specifically. While not always appropriate I often talk with their parents about them while they are within earshot. This communicates two important things to our Grandkids. One is just how significant they are to me and their parents, and second, they know that the adults are singing from the same hymnal when it comes to what they are up to. Not a bad strategy if I do say so myself.

Your reminder pages of each child are for your eyes only so you can jot down anything that you feel is important. It can start with the simple stuff. Date of birth, school and contact information, teachers name, etc. One of my most useful connecting devices is to find out each Grandchild's best friend and why they think of them as best friends. (Tip: leave room or write it in pencil, this one tends to change as they grow, move, etc.) You can also include stuff that is age appropriate. If they are younger you may keep up with their favorite TV shows, Super Heros, etc. As they get older, their favorite music and Popstars. Projecting forward, New Boy/Girlfriend, Video Games, etc. You get the idea.

Keep in mind that, just like the best friends, as they grow these things change. With some of my Grandkids, these things change quite frequently. This is one of those deals where the more you put into your book, the greater and more comfortable the conversation is, especially when they go through the dreaded (Preteen) one-word answer phase.

Your "Treasure Trove" may look like this; For more ideas, stories, and articles you can go to GoodtoGreatGrandparenting.com and look under the You as Grandparent tab.

1. Name (nicknames, which may change as they grow)

2. Birthday (I put the year so I can remember how old they are later. It is a

major faux pax to ask them if they are 14, when they're already 15.

3. What kind of stuff are they Interested in? (this will change with age)

4. Friends (especially the present best friend (BFF) and/or Boy/Girlfriend)

Note: Write in pencil or leave lots of lines in between, these things tend to change a lot.

5. Some of the thing(s) that are unique about them. Characteristics, awards, etc. I often have to stop while doing this part and share the same entry in my Gratitude journal.

Let me detour for a moment here to underscore the importance of this point of looking for the positives in our Grandchildren. Admittedly I am a Gratitude kind of guy. I will encourage anyone I meet and especially my Loved ones, to become a "Good Seer and Good Sayer!" Full Stop, period, end of sentence, end of story and any other superlative you can think of! I am convinced this is what we are put here on earth to do. Even Crotchety Ole Charles Dickens had to admit **"No one is useless in this world who lightens the burden of it to anyone else."**

It is amazing what this does for the seer and the seen. This is a good place to remember. People won't long remember what you say but they will remember how you make them feel. What better contribution is there from you to your Grandchildren than this?

In the words of a wise old Cherokee Indian elder to his Grandson, "Always remember to walk the path of Good Medicine and to see the Good reflection in everything that occurs in life. Life is a lesson, and you must learn the lesson well to see your true reflection in the water, as well as in life itself."

One such example happened on an ordinary visit to a Dentist. Many years ago, I was referred to a specialist Dentist for some sort of work. He was a 40ish guy with a positive energy and personality, as was his staff. I asked the assistant about the Doctor, and she mentioned that the picture on the windowsill was of his three teen boys in their Cricket team uniforms. When he returned, she told him about our conversation. Without hesitation he smiled and began a dissertation about the unique qualities of each of those young men complete with accomplishments, hopes and dreams that they had for themselves. It was considerable and detailed. This, mind you, was right on the tip of his tongue right in the middle of his busy workday. You won't be surprised to learn that after he left the room the assistant told me he was like that with the entire staff, and all his patients. I learned later that he is one of the best and most well-liked men in his field. This man is a Life Force and one of the best "Good Seers and Good Sayers" I have ever met.

Back to the list of possible questions.

6. Areas of concern in their lives, i.e. Health, family moves, parental issues, school changes and challenges such as bullying, number and quality of Friends), etc. Keep in mind this is for your eyes only.

There tends to be a correlation between how much information you gather and your Grandchild's sense of you being present in their lives, for communication and visits with them. More on this in Chapter 3 As a teaser, let me just say that this may have something to do with why Dale Carnegie sold over 30 million copies of "How to Win Friends and Influence People".

Hopefully you now have a new "You are Here/We are Here" starting point. Now with your sense of how you would like to address this Journey I would like to zero in on the concept of mindset. I am sure that by now you are getting the whole "It ain't like it used to be" idea. If we approach our role as Grandparent with a sense of Thoughtfulness and remain aware of the who,

21

what, where, and why of our extended family, we will be assured of a much better outcome.

With this approach we stand a much better chance of not wasting our well-earned wisdom, not squandering our chance to Love our Grandchildren, and enjoying a much more fulfilling experience as a Great Grandparent.

Chapter 2

NEW GRANDPARENTS
(This Changes Everything)

> "Perfect Love sometimes does not come until that first Grandchild."
>
> Welch proverb

Part 1: How We React.

Much like a spectacular Sunrise, becoming a New Grandparent is the beginning of a new day, a new chapter in your life, a completely new role in your family. I clearly remember that my experience was that of a brand-new kind of Love all wrapped up in Joy and Awe. What I find special is that this repeats itself with each new grandchild. Then again with each Great Grandchild, and now with my first Great-Great Grandchild. This is the kind of miracle that never gets old. One wise Grandparent was heard to say, "There will never be a day like the day your Grandchild was born." Oh, Happy Days!

Your Journey doesn't begin at the actual birth. You don't have to like what I am about to say but I would consider it and check it out for yourself before you cross any bridges that you can't get back over. As is true in many families there often is a lot of water that has already passed over the dam before this blessed event. First, we must raise our children and the parents of our new in-laws must raise their children. Even in the best of cases, this cannot be done without a few bruises to the egos of all involved. Now that is an understatement, if ever there was one.

Regardless of how well or badly that phase of life went, it is time to change gears. This juncture requires a total reset. Some of these resets will be harder than others but the outcome of your Grandparenting experience depends on your tuning into this reset. If you keep doing what you have always done, you will keep on getting what you have already got. This blessed event calls for a new level of doing things. Remember the New Day idea.

These two are a couple of young people on the eve of becoming parents. They are as insecure about this monumental leap in life experience as most of us are. They are full of Hope and Fear while at the same time craving approval, as we all did. I don't know about you, but I wasn't an "I've-got-this" kind of guy. When they put my own squirming, crying, absolutely perfect little baby boy in my arms, those arms were trembling, but also sensing what a miracle this was. This changes everything in the parent-child relationship. That is true for the parents of this new baby and for the parents of these grown children about to become parents. This evolution of roles is necessary and inevitable. You raised them to be responsible and now it is time to let go of the bicycle seat and watch them go and grow.

I liken becoming a Grandparent for the first time to setting the Thanksgiving table for the arrival of the extended family. I remember that it was important that the napkins be folded just so. It was important that the glasses be spotless, and the seating arrangement was just right. It was however not important that I understood the whys and wherefores, it was only important that I did it the way Mom asked me to do it.

I was involved because it was my family, but I definitely wasn't the one calling the shots. It is exactly that way when a couple are having their first and subsequent children of their own. They are the parents of these new human beings and while we are part of the family, we are NOT calling the shots.

The birth of that first Grandchild is a major event for all concerned. Your family expands and so does everyone's role, especially yours. Your rewards will be proportionate to your intentionality and considered understanding of family dynamics multiplied by your willingness and ability to thoughtfully engage when and where appropriate. The potential influence you will have on your family is huge. This is your chance to shine once more in an entirely different way. You have joined a unique and consequential club. The stage is yours. Welcome to Grandma and Grandpahood.

This is a critical juncture in the extended family formation and chances for long and harmonious family life. I promise you, that is not hyperbole. That is not an overstatement. Oh, but you say, it is different in our family. Maybe, just maybe so but, statistically over half of the Grandparents don't listen to and/or act on the new parents' wishes. Not such good odds for harmony in the future.

My intention here is not to lick all the red off the peppermint candy of this delicious moment, it is merely to raise up one very significant idea that has so much to do with how an extended family moves forward, or not. It has everything to do with things like your future visitation rights. It has everything to do with what baggage has been brought into this moment from conflicts the parents had with their then rebellious children. It has everything to do with new parents, in a highly emotionally charged atmosphere, not feeling as though you take them seriously. It has everything to do with Respect for their role as parents.

It has been my sad experience to have grieving Grandparents telling stories, after the fact, about how they don't get to see their Grandkids anymore. I hope I have pounded this point into your consciousness. This is the only chance you will have to get this right.

One more try here. The constitution of the United States mentions parents' rights in four different places, there are no mentions of Grandparents rights. Enough said, I hope.

Depending on several factors there are many things to consider even at this magic moment of excitement and joy. This is your first chance to try out this new role as a modern-day Grandparent.

One of my teachers, Jim Rohn, once said "Be careful to not weigh Truth on Sincerity scales and Sincerity on Truth scales." There is a nuanced difference that is ever important at this juncture in the Grandparenting Journey.

He expanded this idea by telling a story that I identified with. One of my many work experiences involved my building and owning a Dry-Cleaning Store. I attended the International Fabricare Institute (IFI) and one of the things they taught us about was the delicacy and difficulty of removing all kinds of stains from fine silks.

It seemed that in days gone by if you viewed a sign outside of a Dry-Cleaning store in Italy you would find, only on the best and most trusted establishments the word "Sincera". This word translated to English means Sincere. It seems that using chemicals strong enough to remove some stains on fine silks would cause the color to release and you would have a spot completely devoid of color instead. The "less scrupulous" cleaners would use pastel chalks to cover their mistakes. Then going forward the next cleaner didn't stand a chance of success with that spot. The best establishments initially worked harder and used less aggressive chemicals like seltzer water along with more laborious techniques to lift that soil but did not damage the dyes in these delicate fabrics.

Mr. Rohn then went on to say that while we value sincerity, sometimes people are sincerely wrong. As an example, he said he thought that Adolf Hitler was sincere, albeit sincerely wrong.

This is a touchy subject, I know, but well worth mentioning. Around the time of this blessed event all concerned are operating in an atmosphere of high energy and heightened emotions. This is understandable, but sometimes it causes well-meaning people to act before they consider all the implications.

Under normal circumstances it may be appropriate for Grandparents from out of town to stay with their child and his spouse. With a first baby coming, maybe not so appropriate. It is not for me to say. I only raise the idea that it may be something to discuss ahead of time.

Let's listen in on an all-too-common story surrounding two sets of Grandparents approaching the birth of their first miracle. The maternal Grandparents Bill and Louise live locally, and they've had a really close relationship with their, now 19-year-old, daughter Lucy. The year before, when their daughter came home to announce that she and Andy were engaged after a short and sometimes tumultuous courtship, they feigned excitement and approval. In the privacy of their own home, however, they often wondered out loud how this whole thing would work. But they remained quiet about it. Their daughter was determined so they went along.

Their fun-loving future son in-laws' parents Carl and Mindy were nice enough but the kind of people who would whisk into town for a quick visit with the newly married kids and a dinner with their daughter in-laws' parents. The talk was jovial but didn't land as meaningful and sincere, however, once again Bill and Louise, behind closed doors, were concerned.

As the birth event approached his parents again whisked into town to stay at their son's home without checking ahead to see if that was okay. Andy merely announced to Lucy that they were coming to stay with them for a couple of days. He made this announcement as they were on the way to the hospital for the delivery. Lucy had too much going on to challenge this, but she did feel uneasy and left out of the conversation.

Everyone rushed to the hospital only to endure a long and difficult labor of nearly 12 hours. Louise was glued to her daughter's side with concern and sympathy while Lucy's father was pacing the floor in the waiting room with equal concern. Meanwhile Carl and Mindy were in and out and obviously annoyed that this was taking so long. As the birth approached Mindy inserted herself into the conversation to say she wanted to be in the delivery room as well. She stated as her reason that this was her first Grandchild too. This time Lucy told her mother that she didn't want anyone but her mother and her husband in the delivery room. You could feel the tension building, as seeds of resentment were being planted.

Now Louise, Lucy's gentle Mom, was being tasked with telling Mindy that her daughter didn't want anyone but her own mother and her husband Andy in the delivery room. This added to the drama of a concerned mother and a now indignant mother in-law at an event steeped in fatigue and emotion, and at a critical juncture in everyone's life. Clueless, father in-law Carl just wants to know what the big deal is.

It is, unfortunately, stories like this that can suck the miracle part right out of the miracle of the first Grandchild. My point is that this is something, no matter the difficulty, that needs to be talked about ahead of time. Mark my words, this is a time in this and everyone's family life that sets the tone for how the family will function, or not, going forward.

Good To Great Grandparenting

The essential thought is to **consider.** It will serve you well to carefully consider the parents' wishes as well as their often sleep-deprived state of anxiety and feeling emotionally overwhelmed. It is also important to consider your relationship, especially with the mother of this miracle. It is normal for the new mother to want her own Mom to be close for this event, but after that the picture is not so clear. It serves all to talk about this openly before the event. If you are the Maternal Grandma, you may be a bit closer to the mother than the Paternal Grandma. While everyone wants to rush in, it is important to offer support but lay back a bit until the appropriate time to be invited in. Please consider that your enthusiasm and willingness to help may be more about satisfying your own desire to connect with this new bundle of joy, and not so much about the new family. Emotions are high and memories are long lasting. There will be plenty of bonding time to come and enough Love to go around. One last time, I urge you to consider the importance of this monumental family event.

A brief word about Grandpas here. Please don't shoot the messenger. It has been my experience that we are normally invited to step back, support, and wait our turn, which may be months or even years, but our time will come and when it does, it is worth the wait. Think of it like fishing, sometimes you just have to wait it out. As I am writing this, I am reading a Great book by one of the leading experts in this field, Richard Eyre called "BEING A PROACTIVE GRANDFATHER". This may help with the "being patient" part.

Each circumstance and every family will differ from the next. I have a friend whose daughter wouldn't allow anyone but her Mom to be with her for her first birthing experience. By the second and third one she LET her husband in in the delivery room with her and her Mom, by the time she was about to have her fourth child she told her Mom that she only wanted her husband in the delivery room this time so the two of them could spend those first moments bonding with **their** baby.

Grandma was a bit taken aback but here we are and again it is **their** baby. Wishing it were different won't make it better, and well-intentioned interjections just add tension to an already emotional and personal event. This is one of those "discretion is the better part of valor" moments.

The ideal scenario is that, as a family, you have planned and talked through the various possibilities. Most of the stories I hear don't include this part of the process. Sometimes as families we don't communicate as well as we would like. In those cases, it is wise to consider the emotionally charged atmosphere, the family hierarchy as well as the various personalities involved before you act. A huge dose of empathy and understanding is the best guide. I have had, primarily Grandfathers, tell me that they just stand back, observe, support where necessary and wait for the halfway mark of this marathon of being a Good Grandparent to assert their influence. This may involve fishing or Monster trucks or a ball and bat, but your time will come. That sounds like wisdom to me.

This momentous occasion of becoming a first time Grandparent is alive with Hope, Gratitude and Possibilities. Celebrate your unique position of influence. You have earned it. You have it in your power to add something to your family that no one else can add. The magic is that the more you add the more everyone benefits, including you. Ain't Life Grand?

Enough about the import of this one major family event. Now comes the best part. We get to use our Superpowers as Grandparents to help this little miracle grow and thrive to become a Loving and Lovable member of our family. Hopefully we have weathered the first part of this Journey with a minimum of battle scars and hurt feelings. Now the fun begins.

During the early days after the mom comes home with her precious baby, there are some unique opportunities to build relationships that will sustain a long and fruitful relationship with your Grandchildren in the years to come. It is common to offer nonspecific help. Many will say to the young couple,

"Let us know if you need anything."

Guess what? They don't even know what they don't know. This is a "first" for all concerned.

Depending upon your relationship, you might offer something specific. You could offer to bring a meal one night a week. Alternatively, now with Grocery stores that offer online shopping along with your choice of pick-up or delivery, you may offer to stop by the store and pick up the groceries, and/or offer to put newly arrived groceries away. In the case of a working Dad, you might offer to cut the grass, run errands, etc.

When the baby gets older you may offer to babysit now and then to let Mom and/or Dad get some much-needed sleep. If this is when the baby is still small you may need some help making sure you have the right stuff in your own home to make it a place that Mom feels comfortable leaving her child. There is the issue of a bed for the new baby. The way a baby sleeps has been updated and the old drop side crib in the attic is no longer the way to go. Things like diapers, wipes, and changing tables are part of the process. If the child is crawling there are a myriad of child proofing techniques to keep them safe. The bottom line is that it is wise to make your home a place which makes it easy for Mom and Dad to bring your Grandchildren.

Part 2: You have come a long way, Baby.

This section will help us learn and reflect on how things, especially those involving the safety and health of this newborn baby, have improved since we ourselves were parents for the first time. Just refer to my earlier story about traveling with my then small chatterbox son. It starts with the times we find ourselves in. It starts with you getting all the appropriate vaccinations weeks before you are going to be around that little bundle of Joy. As a matter of fact, even if you are going to be around those who are going to be around your new Grandchild. Most hospitals won't even let you in their Pediatric waiting rooms without a mask and you being current on your vaccines to protect this precious life.

Now is the time to get a fresh cup of coffee or tea and prepare for some enlightenment about taking care of a newborn in today's much more well-informed world of statistics and medical discoveries.

Just in case you have any doubts about all of this change let me paint a picture of today's newborn's surroundings. These new ways of doing things are not intended to be all inclusive, my hope is to alert you to some of the changes, in an effort to steer you toward doing your own research. This will probably not feel the same as it did for your Grandparents. To begin with, for the first 6 mos. to a year you will step into the parent's room to observe a newborn sleeping on a firm mattress fitted tight to the crib walls. Your newborn Grandchild will be sleeping on their back with nothing else in the crib. For warmth they may be fitted snugly into what is called a sleep sack. No pillow, no toys, no cover sheet. Why, you ask? According to the most recent statistics, statistics; SIDS (Sudden Infant Death Syndrome) rates declined considerably from 130.3 deaths per 100,000 live births in 1990 to 38.4 deaths per 100,000 live births in 2020.

Admittedly SIDS is still somewhat of a mystery, but the most dramatic change since 1990 is the conditions of how newborn babies are sleeping. Now if that change alone doesn't cause you to understand that this baby stuff has come a long way, I suggest you close this book and go cut the grass or do the dishes. I don't think you are ready for this Grandparenting with Greatness thing.

Sorry for the sarcasm but as you just read, this newfound knowledge is very real, and the outcomes are worth the effort to learn all you can on behalf of the safety of your new Grandchild. Besides, as you may have surmised by now, I take this Grandparenting thing very seriously. If you find this sleeping change a shocker, just wait until you get to the whole having to have a PhD in cars seats and a whole village of people willing to spend a half a day on Saturday to help you install the thing.

Just like with sleeping, there are many changes in baby care that are important as well. Not all parents even practice all of these but it is good to have this conversation. A simple, "I realize that things are different now. Can you help me understand the best practices for---- with your new baby".

Some other outstanding things we can do to keep ourselves and our Grandchild safe are things like taking a CPR/Choking course at your local Red Cross. This is important before they come to spend the night or extended babysitting stints. I took my entire Youth Group to a Red Cross training, and they appreciated it and took it seriously. You only need it once to be glad you took it. At the very least there are some effective YouTube videos on this subject. It will be helpful to vet these since there are good and bad ones. Not foolproof but you can usually tell by the number of views they have.

My research has led me to a fact that even I found astounding. Did you know that there are now Non-toxic Baby Powders? It seems that baby Powder can cause breathing issues and lung damage in those teeny tiny lungs of our little cherubs. Once again, do your research and check with Mom.

Now that my kids are grown, I tell the tale of them when they were very small. They were born 1 year and 4 days apart. (Yeah, I know). My son first and his sister the next year. My memory was that one of them slept through the night and one didn't. I told their mom not to remind me which one, because I wanted to Love them equally. I say that tongue-in-cheek, but there were many nights that sleep was at a premium and my wife and I shared the duties equally. As an aside I will tell you that there were more than a few very early mornings when I drove them around in the car and if they fell asleep, I just pulled into the driveway, leaned the seat back and took a catnap.

There was Noooooo way I was risking waking them by taking them into their beds. Okay, I was not a Great Dad, but I was a Good one.

I tell that story about myself to raise awareness of another practice that quite a few new mothers have. It has to do with feeding. This is one of the areas where parents and Grandparents disagree a lot. I defer to the AAP (American Academy of Pediatrics) here.

One of the practices that comes to mind when I tell my ride-around all-night story, is that one trend is that Mothers set a schedule to feed and even if they have to wake the baby up to feed them, they do. Now you can imagine that a man who went through those night rides thinks this is bonkers but then I am not the mother and I have no place doing anything but what the new mother thinks is best. I think this is a Duct Tape moment for me.

The whole feeding thing is a science of its own. I am just here to follow what Mom says. Each child is different, as is each mother. I will suggest that when it comes to things like choking that you pay close attention. I was a bit surprised to find things like marshmallows and peanut butter on the list. Worry not, Mom will have a good list for you.

It is not my intention to scare any of you concerned Grandparents. I only wish to raise some of these things that will help you do your own research into this stuff. I am only skimming the surface to allow you to consider the best way to be an effective Grandparent. Just to let you know that this author made a lot of mistakes, even though I was a very involved parent with the best of intentions. I guess we are back to this Sincerity thing again. I think knowledge is the best antidote for the best outcomes. That is why I have included this chapter for you.

As our wee little ones grow, so does the list of things they can get into. I consider this the pre-crawl stage, the post-crawl stage, the upright and climbing stage and the out-of-control stage. At one of those, Jack Canfield Self Esteem seminars, Jack told of some Graduate students that conducted a survey of toddlers. It seems that a caregiver must deliver 14, no's, look-outs, don't touch that, it's hot, etc. for every positive yes, you can touch that, just to keep them alive. I find that instructive and fascinating at the same time.

You can actually have some fun with this. Your spouse may confirm what he/she already knew and assume that you have lost your ever-loving mind. However, I digress once again. One of the best methods of Grandchild curiosity prevention is to get all the way down to their cheek on the floor level. When they are learning to crawl you just get down on the floor with a flashlight and look from their view. You may not be surprised to find things under the couch that they can pick up and, you guessed it, stuff right into their mouths. At this stage they can reach wall plugs. Off to the hardware store for plug covers. I am telling you it just keeps getting better. I will bet you never even considering having to screw your bookshelves, chest of drawers, etc. to the wall. Welcome to Grandparenthood. Many people miss the kitchen oven door trick. For every stove there is an anti-tip device which can be installed under the stove so that curious climbers can't stand on the oven door and tip the stove forward. See? I told you that you would get a kick out of this Journey.

I may comment on this in jest, but it is a very serious task. A couple of oft-overlooked things about those crawlers is dropped pills from your medicines. You guessed it, right into the mouth. Even the most diligent observer could miss these fast hands when they get hold of a colorful pill. The other is the dog dish of water. Pediatricians say that a small child can drown in as little as 2 inches of water. The list is long and important. My hope is that you can get back up after being down on the floor for so long.

The reason for these cautionary notes is to let you know that it is almost impossible for you to have too much conversation with these new parents about this new addition to the family. I know you want the best for your whole family and specifically for this new member. You have plans for trips, activities, celebrations, etc. with this Grandchild. Your first job is to work diligently with the parents to help them safely grow and prosper. As you will recall, the health and safety of our Grandchildren remains our number one concern.

Chapter 3

LASTING MEANINGFUL CONNECTIONS
(Meet Them Where They Are)

> "Grandchildren are the dots that connect the lines from generation to generation."
>
> Lois Wyse

This chapter is my WHY. It is why I wrote this book. My research and experience have led me to the realization that, left to its own devices, Grandparenting may happen but at nowhere near the deepest and most effective level that it will happen with your intentional participation and effort.

There are things to learn and things to do to ensure a much better outcome for your relationships with each of your Grandchildren. Just getting this far into the book tells me that we are on the same page with hoping for value-added time with and for our Grandkids.

There are time-tested as well as newly discovered best practices that will help us improve the odds of this happening. Let's start with practice number one.

In his iconic book "How to Win Friends and Influence People," Dale Carnegie laid out 6 Ways to make people like you. Principle #5 is "Talk in terms of the other person's interests."

In the 10 years and dozens of trainings I spent assisting a couple who were long-time friends with their franchise for Dale Carnegie Training all over Western North Carolina, I came away with what has become my Life's Goal. To meaningfully connect with as many people as I possibly can anywhere and everywhere. Many people take Dale Carnegie courses to learn about Public Speaking, and rightfully so. My takeaway from those many years is that it was much more about connecting with people. Leaving everyone you meet with more than they had when you met them. I have applied this to my Journey from Good to Great Grandparenting and it is the fundamental inspiration for my writing this book.

There are three surefire ways to get someone where you want them to be. You can push them, pull them, or help them to want to be where you would like them to be.

Mr. Rogers said, "There is a world of difference between insisting on someone's doing something and establishing an atmosphere in which that person can grow into wanting to do it."

When I was a youth minister, I was blessed with a couple dozen extraordinarily beautiful, open, spiritual, and pretty well-behaved teenagers. Most of us had been together for over three years. I knew them and they knew and trusted me. I had promised my then 7th-grade son that I would remove myself as Youth Minister when he got old enough to join the group to allow him to experience someone other than his own parent as his youth minister in this important time of his life. We were approaching that time.

I had planned one last early spring retreat with my kids at the Appalachian Trail Hostel in beautiful Hot Springs, North Carolina. As the date for the retreat approached, we got a new priest assigned to our parish. I had enjoyed the full support of the previous pastor and the parents during the entire tenure of my Ministry. The new priest's reputation preceded him. He was, to put it kindly, old school in a "You shall Obey!' kind of way. Let's just say he didn't understand how I conducted my youth group. I did the best I could to honor his authority and requests, but it was getting increasingly harder. On the eve of our last trip as a group together he called me at home to give me instructions on how to do things. I listened to him patiently. One of his last admonitions was, and I quote "Mr. Taft, I want you to make those young people obey the word of God' I paused and pondered. My response was, "Father, the best I can do is to try to help them to want to obey the word of God". I then hung up. We had a delightful retreat that was meaningful for all who attended.

He preferred I push and pull. My approach that seemed to be working pretty well with this group of teenagers was to help them to want to. Decades later they would come up to me with their "Do you remember when we did this or that?" Those were great times. Mission accomplished.

I tell this story because it is my experience and the teaching of the experts in the area of connecting to today's young people that if you meet them amid their interests and where they are at that point in time, your outcomes will be markedly better when it comes to getting and staying engaged with them.

For simplicity most experts think of Grandkids in four age groupings. We all know that these are kind of squishy ranges but for the sake of discussion let's go with the four age groups. These are 0-2, 3-8, 9-15 and 16 and older.

The 0-2 group is when you get down on the floor with them. They are dependent on us so we just revel in meeting their needs and hoping we can get back up from that floor without the help of another adult. We are prone to making sounds and faces that we don't normally parade in public.

3-8 has to do with learning their interests, albeit changing daily interests at that age. These are the years that we are willing to hold imaginary teacups, endure their tying us up, placing makeup on our faces and wearing silly frilly stuff just to fit into their world. Once again, things we may not exhibit in public. Do I sense a trend here? Remember, we are meeting them where they are.

Between the ages of 9 and 15 a conversation is sometimes harder to come by, their interests are starting to become clearer, and you walk the fine line between them and their parents without overstepping any boundaries. The good thing is that you are still welcome into the world of their friends and classmates.

At 16 and older you marvel at their growth. Though sometimes you hold your breath when they say, Grandma, I want to talk with you about something. This is the time you will have to work harder to enter their world. It is not always easy to understand what they are going through and what they are interested in. Check out the chapter on Social Media for a nugget of knowledge.

Hint: Their parents and keen observation skills are your greatest source of information.

Even though the methods and means change, the basic premise is the same. The closer you operate to their interests the better the outcomes.

Here is but one example of this approach in action. I have a friend whose family migrated from Poland several years back. Eva is a wonderful young mother of two. Her daughter is 12 and her son is 10. To help her kids assimilate in their new home here in the United States she is encouraging them to read American books in English. She shared with me that she is having a tough time getting her son to read. I told her about what I do for my Grandkids when it comes to reading.

I first try to draw out of them what it is that they are most interested in. There are times when this can be like pulling teeth, so I go to plan B. I talk with their parents about what is going on in their lives now. Then I talk with my Grandchild further and if I sense any enthusiasm about a subject I will search out and pre-read a book on the subject to be sure it is a good book as well as appropriate for them to read. I then order them a copy from Amazon and have it delivered directly to them, "in their name." I then let them know I want to hear what they have to say about the book. Now we have a subject for conversation each time we are together. This is not foolproof, but it usually works pretty well.

Here are a few examples.

I am blessed with a Granddaughter who exhibits maturity and discipline that is extraordinary. At this time, she was 18 and beginning a full-ride scholarship to the North Carolina School of the Arts. Just to put this in context, only 1 in 11 of those who apply even get accepted, much less a full ride. Yes, I admit I am a doting Grandpa. The book I chose for her, and pre-read was "Catherine the Great" by Robert K. Massie. I found common characteristics and a possible role model for her in what she is attempting as a career. She is a Drama Major, and this field requires more diligence and perseverance than most.

For my 16-year-old Step-Granddaughter, I chose "Garden Spells" a debut New York Bestselling novel by Sarah Addison Allen (At 16, she likes fantasy Romance Novels). I found it to be a well written and remarkable read as well.

Finally, for my 14-year-old Step Grandson, who is a math genius and gamer, I chose "The Metaverse" by Matthew Ball. Confession time. This book, while very accurate as to where we are headed as a society, was over my head but it is right on as to what he is studying and where his head is. I then asked him to help me understand things like Blockchain, Gaming terms, etc. Bonus, I learned a lot.

Truthfully, some conversations are tough. One of the great blessings in my life is that 3 of my 8 Grandkids, who live 6 hours away from me, must travel 20 minutes to Church each Sunday morning. It has become their habit to call Grandpa Neil almost every week. My middle Granddaughter usually starts the conversation. When I hear my son's ringtone at 9:45ish on Sunday, I answer, "Well, here is my favorite call of the week."

First of all, it IS my favorite call of the week, and second, that greeting is an affirming statement that covers anyone who is using his phone at that time, including him. Score one for ole Grandpa Neil. However, I digress. The routine is for me to have a couple of minutes with each one of them. Here comes the confession. I came to realize that I had to up my game when my then 9-year-old Grandson got the phone. I don't know about you, but I find it challenging to carry on a sustained conversation with a 9-year-old. Get ready for the one-word answers and the fact that I had to ask 20 questions to keep the conversation going. As a rookie, I always ask, "How is School?" How uninspiring is that to a 9-year-old? It comes across as though Grandpa Neil is speaking Mandarin or something. In retrospect, it is a lazy Grandparent question. I have since learned to ask better questions. There is hope however, as either I am getting better and/or he is growing up.

The conversations started getting better when I learned just a little about computer games and began to ask him to help me with the lingo. I actually remember my first question to him. "Do you play your games with just yourself or do others join you online? Turns out this was the right question. It wasn't instantaneous but it has progressed over the past 5 years to a recent time he and I were riding in the car. His oldest sister had just graduated High School and he asked if he could ride the 4-hour drive home with me. Just the two of us. I, of course, loved that he wanted time with Grandpa. We had a great time and a good conversation the whole way. The culmination of that ride was what he said as we approached the driveway of his home. Unsolicited, he said "Grandpa Neil, I like riding with you because we get to talk about neat stuff. That doesn't always happen when I'm in the car with the whole family." Oh, Happy Day!

I tell this story to illustrate a very important point about this Good to Great Journey. It is exactly that, a Journey. Sometimes it feels like a marathon with slow progress, but if you remain intentional and consistent there is Hope. It is the sum total of getting to know each of your Grandkids and keeping up with where they are at that time. Remember that "Resilience" idea from Jim Collins book "Good to Great"?

Now back to my friend, Eva, and her son Jake. After asking Eva the 20 obligatory questions I found out that Jake is interested in everything about cars. I suggested that Eva ask her husband to try my method of; Read a book, then Buy a book to be delivered in their son's name and then open conversations about it. She reports that so far, we are having some success. As I have found, successful conversations and the connections they foster are much more effective if we meet young people **where they are**. Find their interests and plunder them until you get them talking. Then just sit back and marvel at how wonderful and intelligent your Grandkids are. Odds are you will even learn some things along the way as well.

With little ones it is games, play, rhymes and songs. As they get older it seems to progress to doing things together, letting them help you do things and ice cream. Then it is boys/girls, sports, and activities. Then it is watching them on their devices. (Just kidding. Kinda.)

When my Grandkids were small, I found a fun and unique way to connect with each of them. Grandpa Neil was known as the "King of the Upside-Down Hug". Imagine that I grab my 6-year-old Grandson by his arm and slowly draw him to me; I turn him, grab him by the waist, and still slowly turn him upside down. While I am doing this in slow motion I ask, "Do you know what Grandpa Neil Loves about you?" Now he is vertical upside down and I answer loudly while I shake his lunch out of him "EVERYTHING!". Giggles all around, message delivered!

I understand that this is not for everyone but as proof of my process, almost 30 years later my first Grandson Zak, kiddingly, thank God, asks for his upside-down hug every time I see him. To help you understand the absurdity of this now, Zak, 34 years old, is 6'2" tall and weighs in at 240 pounds. My point is that he and every one of my Grandchildren Loved and still remember their Upside-Down Hugs as well as that Grandpa Neil Loves EVERYTHING about them. Just like a farmer planting, fertilizing and then cultivating seeds.

Some of my Grandpa friends have secret handshakes, woodworking workshops, special fishing holes, bike rides or rides in Grandpa's restored convertible muscle car and things like that.

Grandmas have that warm all-encompassing hug, great cookies, and they seem to ask the right questions without fail. One Grandma puts on Granny camps for a half dozen of her Grandkids at a time. These groups are close together in age and these camps include sleepovers, campfires, storytelling, roasting marshmallows, etc.

One expert, Grandpa Richard Eyre whose book I recommended in the New Grandparent chapter, sends half year birthday letters to all 34 of his Grandchildren. What a novel and impactful idea! The point is that it takes thought and effort to truly connect with your Grandkids in whatever way and at whatever stage they are in. These connections are a way of helping each Grandchild to feel significant. As my "now too big for an Upside-Down Hug" grandson Zak says. "It always made me feel like I was special" and he is right. I can't encourage you enough to find your own special way to connect, it makes them feel like they matter.

I am reminded of our mom, Alice. She always found a way to make each of the four of us kids feel like she liked us best.

Here is another story about how Great this journey can be for those of us that take the effort and care to invest in our meaningful connections with our Grandchildren.

It was 7:30 AM on a Saturday and I had just gotten a call, out of the blue, from my, then, 18-year-old Granddaughter. She called me from a high vantage point on the campus of The University of North Carolina School for the Arts where she was a freshman. Remember, this is my "Catherine the Great" granddaughter. She was bubbling with enthusiasm because she was bundled up in a blanket on a 31-degree morning and had just walked all the way across campus to find the highest vantage point to sit and contemplate an awesome Sunrise. I have chills when I write this. Her first thought was to call Grandpa Neil and share her Joy and Awe about this unusual and powerful moment. I am ecstatic and humbled by this monumental and serendipitous event. To underline the uniqueness of this moment let me set the stage.

Along with several other young ladies from her dormitory at school she had gotten up before dawn to take a friend to the airport. Instead of coming back and going back to sleep, which is what her friends did and would be perfectly normal for her teenage self to do, she chose to go on this adventure. I might add that since she had been away at school, she had not been part of those regular, Sunday, Grandpa Neil calls on the way to church, so it had been just birthday calls from her over the past two years. This calls for another Oh, Happy Day!

There are two reasons I tell you this story in addition to my Cup running Over with Gratitude. The first is that for the past ten years when the kids came to visit me for their annual trip to the beach around the time of her birthday, we always made it a ritual that just she and I would get up predawn, stop at the 24-hour convenience store to get her favorite "Yoohoo Chocolate Milk" and me my coffee. Then we drove the few miles to Wrightsville Beach N.C. for our sunrise, or cloud rise, it didn't matter. This became our special time. Note that I had the presence of mind to include an ocean when I chose a place to live. Smart Grandparenting! The second reason is that this is proof positive of the reward we get as Grandparents for doing the thoughtful things that further this Journey consistently and on purpose.

One of my favorite TV shows is "The Mentalist." The character of Patrick Jane is a consultant to the local police when they have a difficult case. He is paired up with a Detective Lisbon who is bright but soft spoken. She has learned to trust his process, so she gives him plenty of leash to do his thing. Prior to helping the police, he had put himself out there as a "Psychic for hire" until one of his clients committed suicide and he blamed himself. While solving these seemingly impossible cases he is often referred to as a psychic because of what he notices. His standard response is that he is not in fact a psychic. He states that he simply pays attention.

The results of paying attention are remarkable. What better subjects for this kind of laser focused attention than our Grandkids? Just wait until you get to possibly your greatest vehicle for insight, the Social Media chapter later.

A common myth around these Lasting Meaningful Connection is that they just kind of happened. There are some connections, usually early on, when the kids are small and the relationships of their parents are still intact, but if you count on this, in the long run, you will be sorely disappointed. No meaningful relationship worth having just happens. Good relationships are the result of a lot of purposeful effort and good intentions. Life Happens to all of us. Unattended relationships diminish, languish, and eventually disappear.

This Journey, while pregnant with possibility, is simple but not always easy. Consideration of changing norms, the complexity of family life, and understanding where young people spend their time are paramount to making this time in your life as fruitful as possible. The more attention you give to this area of your family the greater your reward.

There is an added benefit to your investment in this process. Young minds adhere so much more to what they see us do than what we say. Grandkids see your attention to them as Love in action. They see You as a shining example of stability, security, and safety to your Grandchildren, and that sends a powerful message. What better image to leave with the ones we love than being a beloved Grandparent?

Before I end this chapter, I would like to address the multiple layers of extended family that some of us find ourselves amid. With the divorce rate being what it is, you will do well to consider your place in the family structure and consider what you can do to increase your chances of not being the Grandparents who got thrown under the bus during the upheaval. This decision will pay enormous benefits for you, your Grandchildren, and the entire family.

When turmoil is going on your greatest weapon is your trusty roll of Duct Tape. You will want to join the chorus of bad mouthing, alienating, justifying, etc. There is another way. I know because it is the way I chose. I first armed myself with my all-powerful question, "How much do you want to pay to be right"? Then when my son and his first wife separated, I continued to treat both him and his estranged wife with the greatest of finesse and respect. To this day, over a decade later, I still talk with and support my ex-daughter-in-law with that same respect. I recognize and affirm her for playing a major role in raising this wonderful Young Lady who is my Granddaughter. I let her know that she is and always has been a really good Mom to my Granddaughter and that I am grateful for that.

Now I know that is not always possible, but in my case, it has been and will continue to be the path I choose. When it comes to this whole extended family piece, I know that it is nigh on impossible to remain objective, but I at least want you to recognize the possibility and consider how you can keep the long game in mind. Most of those 400 articles I wrote on my CaringGrandparent.com site had to do with the heartbreak and fallout of families that could not see their way through this jungle of hurt and alienation.

More on this in a later chapter.

A challenge, staying connected over long distances with your Grandkids.

Luckily, the internet rode in on its proverbial white horse to save the day. Before you burn this book because you think the author is absolutely crazy, please hear me out. One Grandma of meager means finally got together enough money to travel to Australia to visit her son, his wife, and her two Grandkids, 9 and 11. That is a long and expensive trip. Grandma knew that she couldn't do this but maybe every other year. She was sad when it came time to leave knowing it would probably be two more years before she got to see them again. It was the 9-year-old who suggested Grandma get a computer. Terrified, she agreed to try. She got a computer, and with considerable help from friends and family and a truckload of anxiety and frustration, she overcame that barrier and now communicates with the entire family almost daily. She is now a part of her Grandkids growing up. Chalk one up for the computer and another one for her finding a way through her fear and anxiety. She now calls herself Computer Granny. My hat is off to her.

One of the most challenging situations for Grandparents is staying connected when the family doesn't live nearby. Grandparenting at a distance requires a whole new set of skills for a great many Grandparents. Often Grandparents tell me this is the part that seems akin to mountain climbing. It usually entails Grandparents' interaction with computers and those scary things called Social Media platforms. In this sense, Covid provided us with what I call the incentive to change. With long terms of isolation and being apart from their Grandchildren, many more Grandparents learned very quickly how to Zoom, Text, etc. I am not sure some of us would have embraced our electronics as swiftly, even eagerly, had it not been for the opportunity to interact with our Grandkids. Interestingly enough, I turned to my Grandchildren to teach me what I needed to know about these new ways of connecting. A bonus was that I allowed my Grandkids to lead me to the appropriate channels and etiquette for online communications with them. For instance, my beautiful Granddaughter told me about Instagram. While foreign to me this is a place where they spend a considerable amount of time. Later in this book, there is an entire chapter dedicated to all things Social Media. It will deal with the appropriate behaviors for Grandparents' and Grandchildren's safety online.

There is a science, if you will, to connections at a long distance that are meaningful and lasting. We have all heard of Long-distance relationships that have stood the test of time. Let's look at increasing the odds that this can happen with your Grandchildren who are not nearby. Some Grandparents only get to travel to see their Grandchildren once or twice a year. You can see where this would be challenging. The good news is that there are many things you can do to keep your relationship fresh and keep it going. Let's dive right into what works.

As a Good News/Bad News scenario, it plays out like this. The good news is that there are age-appropriate things that can be accomplished to maintain this connection. The bad news is that you will be required to step up your game with video on the internet and your phone. So, comb your hair, put on your makeup, shave and/or wash your face, and get ready to do this thing.

I will tell you that you will get better and more comfortable as you do this more regularly. You need not worry about your Grandkids; they are all over TikTok with their friends. It is probably you having to catch up with them.

As it turns out video and the internet are a positive game changer. There is no excuse for you and your Grands to not share videos, Facetime, and anything else that helps you stay part of their lives. At the least, you should regularly be scanning their parent's Facebook, or for that matter, if they aren't still on Facebook, scan their other pages to keep up to date with things like children's performances, home runs, soccer wins, etc. Note I said scan. At first, it is advisable to use these platforms and others to learn what your Grandkids are interested in and what they are doing. Please wait until you read the chapter on Social Media before you start interacting with them on these sites. I will go into much more detail about how you can wade into the water of this vast ocean known as the internet and these sites known as Social Media. There is no harm in observing and learning at the same time. If you have any doubts, just ask your Grandchild. They are familiar with everything to do with Social Media already.

Depending upon the age of your Grandchildren, there are games, short clips, and text messages you can send them that won't intrude on their interaction with their friends on these various sites. One of the most effective methods of connection is to Zoom with them on a regular basis. I can tell you that if you make the effort to reach out to stay connected this sends a very positive message to your Grandchildren that you are interested in them, and they will undoubtedly help you learn what you need to know about what and where they are on the internet.

When I wrote the chapter on Social Media, I was feeling a bit vulnerable since that has not been my go-to place for communications with my village. So, I did my research and then I reached out to my 18-year-old Granddaughter for a quick tutorial on what I wanted to write about. Armed with this information, a couple of interviews and my research I wrote the chapter. I then ran it by her, and she sent me her seal of approval on accuracy and interest. Gee, I passed the test, I am self-impressed.

There is one particularly effective expert in the area of Staying Connected. She is a Young Lady I mentioned elsewhere in this book. Her name is Dr. Kerry Byrne. She has a Master Class titled, appropriately, Grandparenting from a Distance. She is also an expert in the area of Aging, Care, and Connection. She has all the tools and can explain it infinitely better than I do. Check her out at ThelongdistanceGrandparent.com. I found Dr. Byrne to be amongst the most knowledgeable and creative persons in the entire Grandparenting Universe, even though she isn't a Grandparent yet. She has two young children of her own. I have learned so much and am fascinated by her depth of practical resourcefulness.

To stay connected is simple but not necessarily easy. We must learn new things and be consistent and persistent. Some things hit the mark, and some don't. This is the way we find the best ways to stay connected, especially as they grow and change right before our eyes.

Just like the whole Good to Great Journey, it is a Journey worth taking. One very counter intuitive method of staying in touch is by snail mail. I mention this elsewhere, but it is worth repeating because it lends itself to standing out in the throng of stuff kids see every day. I learned this in marketing. If you make it attractive, if you make it lumpy, if you make it stand out with your Grandchild's favorite color, Superhero or Cartoon character it will be opened and read. The bonus is that it will be obvious to them that you cared enough to make it personal. Give it a try and see what you think.

Chapter 4

EFFECTIVENESS
(Playing to Their Strengths)

> "Hope is a waking dream."
>
> Aristotle

A part of our earned wisdom informs us that it is just as important to consider how we impart our stories, experiences, and wisdom as it is what those stories, experiences, and words of wisdom are.

As Grandparents, we are poised to add something to the lives of our Grandchildren that no one else can. Our position offers us a chance to change the lives of our family members throughout the entire extended family. This is not hyperbole; this is destiny if we choose our path wisely.

This is our chance to bring to life all of those Hopes and Dreams to become the best Grandparents we choose to be. This is our chance to keep alive those Hopes and Dreams that our Young Grandchildren have and help them keep those Hopes and Dreams in sight through life's turbulence.

My guess is that you are reading this in hopes of becoming and remaining a powerful force for good in the lives of your Grandchildren. The fact that I separate becoming and remaining a powerful force is to emphasize that they

Neil Taft

are two separate tasks. Much of what you will read in this book has to do with the maintenance of our relationships with our Grandchildren. This is an area of consideration that is often overlooked but is essential to everything about being a Great Grandparent. To be most effective in this journey we will be called upon to be constantly vigilant of all the forces that are happening in the lives of our Grandchildren. This includes the sometimes-complicated forces in the entire extended family.

These pages are intended to offer a glimpse of some of these forces. I apologize in advance that some are terribly messy and even ugly, but we would be derelict if we didn't consider all of them. This is, after all, an extended family we are talking about here and very few of the members were of our choosing. The great news is that the vast majority of Grandparent/Grandchild relationships are chugging right along nicely. That is not to say that even those are not in need of improvement and/or maintenance.

My research has uncovered many important characteristics of the most effective Grandparents operating in the 21st century. Two that stand out are Thoughtfulness, and the use of the power of Hopes and Dreams. This book deals extensively with what I have coined as "Food for Thoughtfulness". This idea is perhaps the most nutritious food of all. This idea has the best chance of operating within that complex structure we call extended family, in such a way that allows us to maintain our Meaningful Lasting Connections to our Grandchildren, through thick and thin.

In this chapter, I hope to set the stage for a deeper meaning and connection with a discussion of the power of Hopes and Dreams. I also have heard from many Grandparents that there are two important elements to these Hopes and Dreams. One is what you have just spent the first chapter working on, your own Hopes and Dreams. The other is Hopes and Dreams as a powerful tool of communication with our Grandchildren. Not just the fluff stuff but

54

the "Man in the Arena" types of Hopes and Dreams that Theodore Roosevelt talked about.

Please don't just skip over the idea of focusing in on this as a tool of communication. Here is where you can plant a most fruitful seed for the future of those you hold most dear. It is impossible to hold a positive and negative thought in your mind at the same time. I choose positive thoughts for my journey. I choose positive thoughts for my Grandchildren.

I am an optimist. Even at almost 80 years old my fuel is still my Hopes and Dreams. I sit at this keyboard at 4AM as an expression of the power behind that very tool. I look into those bright and shining eyes of my Grandchildren when I get them talking about who they want to become. Their Hopes and Dreams are the bright and shining beacons in the darkness. Within those Hopes and Dreams is what they want to accomplish in life. I know first-hand the energy created by looking forward. We share stories of those who have gone before us. We share stories of overcoming some challenging barriers. We talk about things like resilience.

Just think about how powerful and inspiring it is to sit with our Hopes and Dreams. Our earned wisdom informs us that we become what we think about. It is so powerful to think about these things with our Grandchildren. It, in effect, gives them permission to think big, to hope big, and to dream big. This is a great way to raise those possibilities. To raise up those bright and shining beacons in the darkness. To empower them to be the light they are seeking.

Here is a partial list of some of the positive outcomes of conversations focused on Hopes and Dreams.

They guide and motivate young minds. They will act as guiding stars, illuminating a path we choose. This can be a path to learning new skills and doing things that are a bit scary. A path all the way to choosing and building a fulfilling career. Keeping our vision in our minds fuels our motivation and keeps us moving forward, even on that bumpy dirt road to the mine of our goals.

Resilience and Sticktoitiveness. When life inevitably throws us curve balls, and erects roadblocks, we can hold onto these Hopes and Dreams to get us through. You know, the ole "Pick yourself up and dust yourself off" deal. Most times folks emerge even stronger and more determined. This is the kind of idea I want to help my Grandchildren to focus on. This idea was important enough for Jim Collins to write a most successful business book about it. Hopes and Dreams are worth "Building ideas that Last." This is the idea of knowing there is something better to come. I would go so far as to call it an antidote to all the STUFF going on in today's world. Our children are not immune to that stuff, but we can sure give them something better to aim for.

Passion and Creativity are offshoots of holding Hopes and Dreams at the top of the mind. Dreams help to push the boundaries of the possible. Dreams break down perceived limitations; they fuel and generate an atmosphere of creativity that leads to groundbreaking ideas, inventions, and growth in general. Everything, let me repeat, EVERYTHING began as an idea in one person's mind. I am in absolute awe every time I write that sentence. I find that my Grandchildren react much the same way. Why not plant this kind of possibility thinking by helping them articulate their own Hopes and Dreams? The two most helpful things you can contribute are to be present to them and ask more thoughtful questions.

Hopes and Dreams foster meaning and purpose in lives. Isn't this foundational to them walking in this sometimes cold and indifferent world? Isn't this what is connecting us to our highest and best selves? Isn't this our Superpower as a Grandparent?

Connection, connection, and connection. When we are sharing Hopes and Dreams, we tend to attract others that do the same. One of my teachers once verbalized the finding that we become like those we hang around with. It is a reciprocal synergistic exchange of the best kind that creates positive energy for all involved. Often subtle and hard to quantify but the movement is in the right direction. It fosters a sense of common ground and feeling of belonging.

Hold onto your Hopes and Dreams and find the way into eliciting what your Grandchildren are Hoping and Dreaming about and do all you can to keep that conversation going as they grow. Some of their Dreams may change but that also is progress towards who they wish to become. These kinds of conversation, while requiring a lot of thought on your part, are an antidote to all this STUFF going on around us,

Let me close this chapter with some "Food for thoughtfulness". Socrates taught us that the quality of our questions will determine so much. Jean Nidetch offers "Choice not chance determines your destiny" I vote for choosing our questions wisely when we have our Grandchildren's attention. By working within this Hope and keeping our Dreams in sight we can inspire our Grandchildren to thrive.

Chapter 5

LIVING OUR VALUES

> "What you do speaks so loud I can't hear what you are saying."
>
> Ralph Waldo Emerson

The fact that you are still reading this book lets me know that I am somewhat preaching to the choir when it comes to living our values. I am not worried that you are lacking intention, but I do think it is important to consider how we share our values with our Grandkids. It is right on target to think that there is a theme of finesse when it comes to us being our best at this Grandparenting deal.

High in the 90 percent range of Caring Grandparents that I have interviewed, have placed the sharing of wisdom as one of their most hoped for contributions that they wish to impart to their Grandchildren. There is no doubt that what they wish to share is earned wisdom. Wisdom born out of blood, sweat, and tears, and now, having persevered, you wish to spare your Grandkids the pain of these lessons. To be clear I am not so naive as to think we can shield them from every trial in life. What I do know is that we can do all in our power to create an atmosphere that helps them want to learn our values before they get into these inevitable situations. One of my teachers would follow a teaching moment with the question, "Now how do you think

I know that?" If you lead with an attitude of vulnerability and humility you have a much better chance of being heard. Heavy on empathy and not so much on preaching. This helps them to know that they are significant.

"Those who have a strong sense of love and belonging have the courage to be imperfect."

- Brene Brown

This section is presented as a way to share some of the things that I know to have worked well and some not so well. I just want you to be aware of some of these possibilities in addition to your own.

I shared the story earlier of the Grandparents that attended the church of the family while visiting them and took the Grandkids with them to their church when they came to stay with Grandma and Grandpa. That story is a two-fer. It demonstrates the value of openness and the value of the importance of faith with a sprinkle of family unity thrown in for good measure.

I also told the story of the priest who asked me to MAKE my youth Group kids obey the word of God. While each of these stories had a message germane to the chapter they were in, I think here they can create a dynamic that may be useful to Grandparents who so desperately want to share their faith with their Grandchildren. Many don't know where to begin, or how to communicate their faith with young people, and in some families, it is seldom talked about. If you are thinking hard about this then my hat is off to you. You have the right mindset for imparting what you find important to be passed onto your Grandkids for their consideration. There, I said it, for their consideration.

To illustrate what I have seen to be most effective when it comes to young people and church, I am willing to go way out on this high dive with my observations.

When children are young it is somewhere between important and essential that they are shown some form of ritual worship. It is equally essential that they find a sense of community, and if that is community worship, that is even more valuable for them. Human connection and belonging are a bonus to young children. If you recall I also told the story of my teenage Grandkids calling me on the way to church on Sunday mornings. At this stage in their lives, they are going because they want to be in the community. Isn't it interesting that this going toward something meaningful brings up the thought of connecting with their ole Grandpa. Just sayin'.

This is what is going on in our family, but I understand that this is not always the case. Faith, community, and church are not always the same thing. I know very few adults and mature adults who have figured this whole faith, community, and church thing out. I have also known some folks who cling so frantically to their own beliefs that they sometimes leave their own children and the rest of the world feeling isolated from that experience. There is no right or wrong approach; just one approach is inclusive, and the other, not so much.

I once dated a lady who invited me to occasional Sunday dinners at her parents' house. The dynamic was interesting, to say the least. The parents had 5 grown kids. Mom and Dad were members of a very fundamentalist faith. Devout and good people. It is instructive that I describe each of their children's responses to religion. In their adult years, one was the peacekeeper, a good and caring woman just like her mother and she was guarded about sharing her faith, one daughter studied to be a Catholic nun, one son was a Seventh-Day Adventist, and the other son stayed home each Sunday morning and drank beer and watched TV while the Lady I was dating would NOT talk to me about religion. Sunday mornings brought tension into our relationship that you could cut with a butter knife. This was what I would refer to as a very dynamic family when it comes to religion and how it manifests itself with some people.

Let me return to the Sunday gatherings. Their dad would sit there, and each of those who entered gave him a Loving hug and hello as he sat with his wife of 60 years, holding hands in their famous side-by-side recliners in the den. The room slowly filled with chatter and friendly folks. I truly felt comfortable there from early on. Some of the now-grown wives and mothers and one son-in-law would drift in and out of the den while keeping an eye on the meal prep duties in the kitchen. When the audience got to near capacity in the den the dad would reach for the remote and turn the channel to a presentation on Prophecy by his favorite preacher and turn the volume up. It was as if it had been scripted; first out of the room were the young people, then the grown kids, and then their spouses/partners. I was the new guy. I didn't know the drill, so I stayed politely glued to my chair as the only one left in the room. You guessed it, the Dad took this as my profound interest in what he had on the TV. Now, I am a slow learner, but over time, I, too, took my cue and exited lest I be served up a 20-minute lecture on the intricacies of Prophecy. This drama played out the same way for years in that little den by this otherwise Loving and close family.

Please don't take this as anything other than a family dynamic that illustrates the point that the way something is presented is very important to how it is or isn't received.

Maybe, just maybe there is a lesson to be learned in human nature. Maybe there is a consideration of how we impart what is important to us in our faith to those we care most about. My admonition is that you give it a lot of thought. You should pray about it long and hard, in an effort to best communicate your values. I am a firm believer that our Grandkids are not apprentice people, they are real little people living and learning. Actually, I have learned to learn from them as well.

As I was planning to step aside as a Youth Leader, I gathered my Youth Group parents for one last meeting about the kids. I was asked an important question by one of the most supportive parents of two of my extraordinary youth group members. The Mom asked, "What are your takeaways from your years as Youth Minister of this group?" My answer came easily, "I learned about my own walk of faith. I learned so much about spirituality and goodness from these kids. I learned to have faith in the future. This experience fueled my Hope gland."

I have carried that knowledge forward into my role as Grandpa. I seldom talk with my Grandchildren about their faith; however, I never miss a chance to affirm the things they are doing to foster that faith. I do, however, ask them about their thoughts on Good and Evil. I do ask them about what community and/or isolation means to them. I do ask them about things they are doing to grow as a Loving and Lovable human being.

"There is no limit to the power of loving."
- John Morton

It is very important that we do our best to help our Grandkids grow morally and spiritually. I do feel that it is our sacred duty to be as effective at communicating this subject as is humanly possible. You will find it much easier and more effective when you can intertwine your moral and spiritual values in the context of meeting them where they are.

Most folks have a pollyannaish view of what to share with their Grandkids. I find there is just as much value in sharing things that didn't work in our lives. This is especially true when they themselves have experienced sadness or setbacks. Empathy is a powerful communicator.

Perfection can be a powerful communication barrier. Teaching moments sometimes hide under rocks in some dark and slimy places. Some of the most interesting discoveries in my life were found under rocks. I don't want to beat this idea to death, but I do want you to consider that while we share noble expectations with them, we don't inadvertently communicate that perfection is either expected or possible.

Being real with our Grandkids is just as important a lesson in values as are the rules and regulations for a better life. Unrealistic expectations can be limiting and/or defeating. Remember Brene Brown's quote about courage and imperfection.

Dr. Charles W. Shedd wrote a lot about the fact that it is not always necessary to teach young adults what is right and wrong, they know that. It is, however, powerful to teach them what is smart.

Some people see this as giving kids permission to fail. I have bad news for those folks, they will fail with or without your permission. The important thing is "It is what they do next that counts."

You will find that if you have done the work that leads to lasting meaningful connection with your Grandchildren then they are eager to hear your stories. Congratulations, you have helped them to want to know and have good values. That is the most effective way to communicate values.

Chapter 6

THE ELEPHANT(S) IN THE ROOM

> "Success is due to our stretching to the challenges of life.
> Failure comes when we shrink from them."
>
> John C. Maxwell

In way too many families there is a branch of the family that is not functioning as hoped. By the nature of the beast, it is not a subject that is talked about openly. I will urge you to at least be aware of what is transpiring in your family. The reality is that it is also transpiring in many extended families. Keep an eye out for the signs of these issues, in the event you can help support those involved and possibly avert them.

The Elephant(s) in the room:

a) Divorce: About half of all first marriages in the United States end in divorce. Another challenge is that nearly 2/3rds of second marriages end in divorce as well. Given that the parents are the chief stewards of our Grandchildren you can see where this has the potential to affect our relationships with our Grandkids. The sad reality is that if you are the paternal Grandparents, unless you do some extraordinary work, the odds are stacked against you. Please keep this in mind when you read the chapter on Alienated Grandparents. Let me tease you here with the best tool you have in your Grandparent's toolbox. That tool is the question "How much do you want to pay to be right?"

b) Drug addiction and all of its ancillary consequences, i.e. Incarceration, abandonment, and drug overdose deaths, which usually take down the other parent eventually. We don't like to talk about it, but this is an epidemic. By definition, an epidemic is a widespread occurrence of an infectious disease in a community at a particular time. This is a particular time, and it is in every community.

c) Controlling spouses/partners. More on this in the next chapter.

The consequences of these issues are far-reaching and devastating to all involved. In many cases you may not be able to head these things off, but you certainly can support all those involved. It is rare that I meet an extended family that hasn't been touched in some way or possibly crushed by the Elephant. The lack of awareness just adds to the shock and disappointment when something like this comes close to you. Lack of awareness can rob you of the ability to offer help and support where possible. Lack of awareness can impact your ability to see your Grandchildren.

Grandparents are often caught unaware and then left to mop up the mess. From a legal standpoint we are in a weird position. From a practical standpoint we are sometimes left in a sad position. There is some hope on the horizon, just recently the courts are finding the Grandparents to be a way through some of these dramas but that has been slow coming and has not always been the case.

I have been a long-time student of Grandparents Rights and Alienated Grandparents. I have written two books on the subject and if I were pressed to define what rights a Grandparent has when it comes to their Grandkids in matters of visitation, guardianship, and connection, I would have to say it is "Slim to None" from a strictly legal standpoint. Having said that and being a Grandparent of Step-Grandchildren and an ex-in-law to the mother of my Granddaughter I am acutely aware of the need to give this area of extended family life a lot of thought. Think in terms of "an ounce of prevention." Function as much as you can like the neutral version of Switzerland.

Just as we are best served to recognize our supporting role to the parents when it comes to the Grandchildren it is even more important to be proactive and intentional when it comes to preserving these valued relationships during turbulent family times and going forward.

There are two really crucial times in a Grandparent's journey that allow us to elevate the relationship with your Grandkids above all else. The first, as I laid out in Chapter 2, is when you are a new Grandparent and emotions are soaring, the second is when your own child is in the middle of his or her own family turmoil and once again...wait for it...the emotions are high.

When that first newborn arrives, you have all of these hopes and dreams and a desire to be the best Grandparent in the world. While at the same time you are having to adjust to letting go of the control of your grown child and allowing the now grown child and their spouse to take the lead and do it their way. This is where your considered ability to finesse comes into play.

There are some differences if you are the maternal or the paternal Grandparents but the overarching principle here is that this is not a competition. This is not an us versus them deal. This is a keep the best interest of the Grandchildren top of mind moment. Wise Grandparents see this as the "Mom and Dad" show with the parents as the ushers. I recognize that this is a tough pill to swallow, but it is a time of significant impact on your future as a Great Grandparent.

As time passes and there is trouble in paradise you understandably want to defend your own child but at what cost? The common denominator in these two critical junctures of Grandparenting is emotion. The paradox is that you can cause yourself as well as your Grandchildren a good deal of heartache while you see yourself as acting with the best of intentions. Keep the "Long Game" front and center, this may be your greatest test. Be careful not to get yourself sidelined at this crucial time in your family. There is a different way to handle these moments. It is probably one of the truly Good to Great moments that pays the greatest benefits to all involved. Let me say once again, I recognize the difficulty of the moment, but I am witness to the import of the moment as well. It warrants your consideration.

Let me throw you a lifeline here. Right now, as you read these lines you can improve your chances of a longer and happier Grandparenthood and as a bonus even the possibility of a happier life overall if you arm yourself with this one question. Before you speak, ask yourself "How much do I want to pay to be right"? Especially if you are paternal grandparents. This can be a most profound decision point in your family. Prepare your mind for the eventuality and choose your Grandchildren. It IS a decision and one not easily taken back.

Ah... BUT! I hear you loud and clear. Please know that I understand that your circumstances may really be dire and unfair. It is not about fairness. I want you to separate the idea of fairness and ask yourself if the job of telling the offending party just how you feel is truly worth the potential result.

Venting your feelings in that moment may turn out to be more important than time with your Grandkids, because often that is exactly the choice you must make in your emotionally charged state of mind.

I am in no way challenging your right to BE right. This is not intended to tell you what to do, it is merely one of the most important decision points of your Grandparenting life and all I suggest is that BEFORE you speak you STOP and ask yourself "How much do I want to pay to be right"?

In my own journey this simple yet profound question has allowed me to have a good, even if at first strained, relationship with the mother of my wonderful Granddaughter over the past dozen years. During my research for this and my other Grandparenting books I have encountered many stories of Grandparents who have one sentence or one encounter with an in-law that they deeply wish they could unsay.

One example is an older couple, Grammy and Paw Paw. Tragically, Grammy and Paw Paw's young Granddaughter died of an overdose soon after giving birth to her first child, Lillie, who was their first Great Grandchild. The baby's biological father was incarcerated and had contributed to that young mother's short, hard life, by subjecting her to domestic violence.

After the death of the mom the courts allowed Grammy and Paw Paw to become Lillie's guardians. They were on cloud nine. It had been several decades since they had the opportunity to shower a little miracle with Love and more Love. As months passed, they took all the steps toward adoption, but the father was defensive. All of this just made Paw Paw angrier. I give Grammy most of the credit, she swallowed her pride and kept the best interest of her Great Grandchild front and center. Finally, after 6 months and many calls to the jail and trips to the courthouse, she talked the father into signing the papers to terminate his parental rights so they could adopt and raise their Lillie in a safe, Loving, and stable home environment.

The day before, let me repeat this, the day before he was to sign those papers, after months of back and forth with lawyers and the courts, Grammy and PawPaw had one last phone call to the jail to finalize a few things with Lillie's biological father. Just before they hung up, Paw Paw couldn't hold back anymore, he just had to tell him what a cruel and no good person he had been to their Granddaughter. That was their last sentence to him. You guessed it. Tragically, he hung up on them and refused to sign the papers and that baby went into the foster care system. Poof! All was lost in one sentence. I wish I could say that this is a fable, but it is a true story that plays out all too often.

The number of Alienated Grandparents is large and growing. This is an extreme case, but still a tragedy on top of a tragedy. We can certainly recognize that these Great Grandparents had the right to speak out, some can say that they were justified.

How much did Paw Paw pay to be right? How much has Lillie paid for him to be right?

Please, please, please, in the name of all things Great about Great Grandparenting, arm yourself with this question or some thought that allows you to preserve this sacred bond you have forged with your Grandkids over the long haul and over these familial bumps in the road.

There is a tool that some Grandparents use to help in these situations. I call it the Metaphorical roll of Duct tape. Each time one of these situations arises, you just tear off an 8" piece of tape and place it across your mouth. Leave it there until the urge to speak subsides.

Over the past dozen years, I have received far too many stories from devastated, brokenhearted Grandparents, some of whom have even raised their young Grandkids, babysat 5 days a week while the parents worked. They fed and loved them for years on end only to have them snatched from their arms and be refused even visitation and contact with them.

A friend of mine, now retired, was a Family Law Attorney in Michigan. Richard S. Victor. He is the founder and executive director of the national nonprofit Grandparents Rights Organization. He is a prominent award-winning champion of Grandparenting. He gave me permission to quote him in both of my earlier books. He stated the situation succinctly; "Remember, if death takes a grandparent from a grandchild, that is a tragedy, but if petty vindictiveness and hostilities within a family amputates a grandchild from their grandparents, then that is a shame."

I hope this helps you be more mindful of how what you say impacts your journey and your Grandchildren's future.

Chapter 7

THE SQUISHY STUFF

> "I'm a participant in the doctrine of constructive ambiguity."
>
> Vernon A. Walters

I debated taking on these two subjects but realized I would not be authentic to my own values and beliefs about Grandparenting, nor fair to you, if I skipped them. I don't expect everyone who reads this chapter to agree, and I am fine with that. What I would hope is that everyone who reads this chapter at least gives what I have to say some thought. These two issues are very nuanced. I present them in the spirit of "Food for Thoughtfulness."

Here goes the two squishiest subjects. They are Spoiling Grandkids and Gift Giving. These are two subjects with a lot of wiggle room. What I hope to share is that there are some lines that should not be crossed. They are not my lines. They are the lines of what parents say about spoiling and in the case of Gifts the lines of the observing experts.

Spoiling

I often check in with my own children about the wellbeing of my Grandkids. I also check to see if there are things that I can be doing to reinforce what is going on in the wonderful world of parenting. Once again, the spectrum is wide, but if you have a close relationship and frequent contact with your children about your Grandchildren I may be preaching to the choir. That does not mean I won't state the obvious lest it be overlooked.

If you google Grandparent's quotes, most are warm and fuzzy. Then you run across a misguided attempt at humor like this.

"The reason grandchildren and grandparents get along so well is that they have a common enemy."

- Sam Levenson

Or

"When grandparents enter the door, discipline flies out the window."

- Ogden Nash

Call me an old fuddy duddy, but if this is a plaque on the wall of a Grandparent's home, my fear is that it becomes counterproductive. I am allowed by my grown children to offer my Grandkids an extra cookie or, my favorite, ice cream, now and then, but I would no more offer them the above idea than I would allow harm to come to them.

This may be stark, but I just want to offer you all a chance to think about what message we are imparting to the minds of those who look up to us. We are full circle back to the word consider.

Before I step down from my soap box, let me address Gift Giving.

In almost every book or article I read about becoming a New Grandparent the idea of Gift Giving comes up. It seems that it often becomes a competition between the Grandparents. The best advice about this is to ask the parents. I don't know of too many 3-month-olds that can benefit from a room full of plastic STUFF. Once again just take a step back and consider.

This penchant for over-the-top Gift Giving has the potential to translate into your Grandchildren later greeting you at the door with "What did you bring us this time Grandma"? Rather than, "It is soooooo good to see you, Grandma". Just sayin'.

Sermon over.

Chapter 8

THE UNIMAGINABLE - Grandchild Abuse and/or Neglect (This Includes Bullying)

> "The difference between something good and something great is attention to detail."
>
> Charles R. Swindoll

I would rather have not been tasked with writing this chapter, but it is definitely way too important to skip. The #1 concern of Grandparents, hands down, is the Health and Safety of their Grandchildren. That coupled with the unique position of Grandparents in the family structure makes this subject not only germane to this book, but it is a way to make this world a better place for all children, especially our own Grandchildren. If you do all you can to create a meaningful lasting relationship with your Grandchildren, then you may be the one SAFE PLACE for this child to turn to if their world goes haywire.

Every 21 minutes a child is abused in this country. This equates to over 25,000 each year. Waaaaay too important to skip. As Grandparents we are in a position to be an early detector. I know, I don't want to think about it either, but I am not making this up. It does happen and as focused observers of our Grandkids, hopefully not, however we just may see some of the early warning signs listed below and be instrumental in saving a child from this experience.

In the first chapter we take stock of each of our Grandkids in what I call the Treasure Trove. Since this is just for your eyes this is a good place to register any concerns about their family situation, changes in behavior, etc. Writing even our suspicions down is a helpful tool if these suspicions ever materialize.

A few things to consider; This is serious territory both from the family relationship perspective and from the consequences for our Grandchildren's safety perspective.

To illustrate what can happen, let me tell you a cautionary tale. When our firstborn was about three or four, he, being the Energizer Bunny that he was and still is over 50 years later, fell off the swing and broke his right ankle. Fortunately, x-rays showed it was not a compound fracture, so the Emergency room Doctor put his right leg in a half cast and sent us back home. We were told to keep him off of it for the next week. Good luck with that.

About two days later he slipped on the Terrazzo floor on the front porch and fell. Back to the emergency room. He was only bruised but no additional bones were broken, and the leg checked out OK.

A few weeks later he slipped while climbing a small and close to the ground tree in our front yard, but his armpit got hung up on a sharp limb stub and he got a fairly significant cut. Back to the Emergency room for a few stitches and an antibiotic. Wait for it...wait for it...

A few days later we were visited by the county health nurse to check on his wellbeing. Fortunately, our home showed no signs of a torture chamber, and it was clean and orderly enough that she went away satisfied that he had not been subject to nightly beatings. In retrospect, we were glad that someone was paying attention, and this was 1972. The good news is that someone WAS paying attention. We should be that someone.

As a Grandparent this puts you squarely in a very powerful position which in some cases may devolve into a delicate situation. If you see some of the signs listed below you have a critical decision to make. If you suspect bullying, it is an easy call to involve the parents. If you suspect abuse at the hands of another family member, then it becomes harder. If you find yourself in this position, please ponder it, pray on it and ponder it some more because it is a bridge that is hard, if not impossible to cross back over.

Having said all of that, the first rule of safety for the child is that if you see something is to report it. If you merely suspect something, document it somewhere, if only your trusty legal pad or Treasure Trove pages. Remember that details count. The suggestion of the experts is that you, at a minimum, tell someone you trust. A family therapist, a doctor, a social worker, or someone from the clergy. If the situation is dangerous, call Child Protective Services or the police. If it is that bad, the prevailing wisdom is, don't confront the abuser. Let the professionals handle it. There is even an option to call anonymously. If you need a trained counselor, call The National Child Abuse Hotline.

This is a function provided by ChildHelp, 1-800-4 A CHILD. 1-800-422-4453. The companion online version of this is www.childhelphotline.org

As a Caring Grandparent some of these signs of abuse and neglect will probably already have been obvious to you but just in case, here they are. These apply to Emotional, Sexual and Physical abuse, as well as Neglect.

1. Changes in behavior. This may manifest as anxiety, not wanting to go home, fear of certain people in or close to the family, even changes in

eating habits.

2. Physical injuries consistent with being severely punished or abused. Things like welts, burn marks or new bruises. Take photos and make notes of dates and particulars.
3. In small children, renewed bed wetting after they have conquered that hurdle.
4. Self-soothing actions, flinching that they never did before or even nail biting that shows up as a new behavior.
5. Extreme cases may involve cutting behaviors.
6. Unusual hunger, poor hygiene, inattention by the caregivers.
7. Isolation
8. Eating disorders.
9. Fear of a certain person or family member.
10. Infections or any genital injuries.

If any of this happens in your family, there are several options for you as a Grandparent.

I would first find a support community to help me through this extremely confusing and disappointing time. One of the best support structure I know can be found Grandparents Raising Grandchildren - HelpGuide.org

This is new territory for most folks and support is paramount to get through it. You are not in this alone, there are tens of thousands that experience this tragedy each year. Facebook has a Grandparents Raising Grandchildren site that has 1600 members. It is a closed group but easy to join.

Other considerations are getting legal help. An article on ModernFamilyLaw.com states; "In today's world of modern families, it's not unusual for grandparents to seek their own rights regarding their grandchildren. This is a well-established statutory ability for grandparents (or great-grandparents). With this ability, grandparents "seek a court order granting them reasonable grandchild or great-grandchild visitation rights. However, the implementation of these rights can only be done when the custody of children becomes an issue before the Courts. Examples of appropriate circumstances would include divorce, allocation of parental responsibilities (custody), and the death of a parent. In some cases, the State steps in to remove the children from the parents for neglect or abuse of the children which act as a situational qualifier. It is important to understand that outside of these circumstances, grandparents do not have the ability or standing to request implementation of grandparents' rights. Absent such circumstances, parents have the right to provide visitation with grandparents as they see fit."

This course of action is more for after the abuse has been reported but staying in touch with your Grandchild is paramount to that child's healing. No matter what it takes, you most probably will be the safest and most effective person in their lives at this point.

Much has been written about the value of a trusted member of the family and for the victims' need to be supported and reminded it is not their fault. Most likely the perpetrator has messed with their minds. Listen, listen, and listen some more. If they aren't communicative then let them know they matter to you and that you are there for them. Whatever it takes to make being with you a safe place for them is the most effective approach.

Usually involving a professional therapist and/or social worker will help support you and the child. Most jurisdictions have a Child Protective Service, even though it may be called by various names. Everything you can do to focus on the child's well-being is a step towards them trusting you and facilitating their healing.

Don't forget you in all of this. The journey back to stability and healing is long, hard and will exact an emotional toll if you don't consider your own well-being. You should take good care of yourself so you can be in it for the long run. You undoubtedly will represent hope, support, and stability for your Grandchild. This may entail you setting boundaries as well. You should build an active support network to help you during this time and going forward.

No matter the personal costs, being an advocate for an abused and/or neglected child is a noble cause. Learn all you can to help your Grandchild and yourself to weather this storm. Regardless of the uphill climb that will ensue, the Journey is definitely worth it.

Chapter 9

ALIENATED GRANDPARENTS
(By Mistake And On purpose)

> "There's nothing written in the Bible, Old or New Testament, that says, 'If you believe in Me, you ain't going to have no troubles."
>
> Ray Charles

Let me remind each of you reading this that the vast, vast majority of families find ways to accommodate even some tough circumstances to maintain good connections to their entire family. My prayer is that if you ever encounter any of these situations, or if it is in a friend's family that you may be able to help by your knowledge of such things. I know I didn't sit down one day and enter into an exercise of "catastrophizing" just to come up with these possible roadblocks to a happy extended family. I did, however, recognize that knowledge is power. It is for that reason that I write about some of these family dilemmas so those who read this and see some of these things coming, will be better able to understand WHAT it is that they are seeing.

My belief is that some of us fall prey to situations that we don't see coming and/or have no control over. To suddenly find ourselves in the middle of one of these circumstances may be too late and/or rob us of our ability to think rationally as to what we can do about it.

I have done a lot of research and spent considerable time and conversations with many who contribute to the Grandparenting space to try to surmise how we got here. Normally that is the foundation of all research.

Please feel free to correct me if I'm wrong, but in this case a few paradoxes may be the best I can come up with.

Let me take a stab at this.

1. I have stated that parent's rights are found in 4 different places in the Constitution, Grandparents zero. If you are a Grandparent, you may wonder things like, "Did they forget"? I doubt it. Just consider that the life expectancy, when this remarkable document was written, in America in 1776 was 35 years old, in 2024 it is 79.
2. We raise our children to be independent, responsible adults yet we have trouble turning over the reins to them, allowing them to be independent and trusting them to be responsible when they have their own children.
3. Great-Grandparents live in a culture of abundance with the lingering memory of the Great Depression. We wanted our kids and their kids to have more and be better off, so we fall into the trap of "spoiling our Grandchildren" while thinking that it's cute. Just sayin'.
4. We have created a society that moves so fast and is so complex that there is a good chance that, like me, we are raising a generation that is more capable in many respects than we are.

How am I doing so far?

My point is that we, the parents, Grandparents, and Great-Grandparents don't come to this with cross purposes. I would proffer that we come at this with the same purpose, the best interest of the Grandchild. It is that we come to this from different focal points, different experiences, and different bodies of knowledge. This is the best of all news; this allows us as

Grandparents to adjust our approach to align with the Parents. This is the essence of the Good to Great Journey. This can be our gift to our family and especially to our Grandchildren.

For the sake of Optimism let me interject a quote from Albert Einstein here; "We cannot solve our problems with the same thinking we used when we created them."

These are not doomsday scenarios; they are merely paradoxes for us to work through. When it comes to paradox, confusion is understandable. We just have to dig deeper and try harder.

It is in your power and mine to reframe the challenge and step up. Because it is complicated, because it is paradoxical, it does not excuse us from applying all of our Superpower (Love) to do what we can, learn what we can to step up our game for the sake of our families and, by extension, the family of this universe. This is not hyperbole. This is where we must begin.

Now back to the task at hand.

Becoming alienated from your Grandchildren is usually through no fault of the Grandparents. I say usually, because there are some things that you can do to increase your odds of this not happening regardless of how alienation comes about, so I would hope you consider these strategies.

The first part of this chapter covers most of the cases where alienation occurs, the second set of circumstances is less hopeful and, finally, the section on prevention is just that. These are the things you should keep in mind when you see the storm building, and things are at a heightened state of emotion; this is when you must reach deep and find an extraordinary power that you may not think you even have.

Good To Great Grandparenting

Alienation from your Grandchildren is an extreme but very possible outcome of The Elephant(s) in the Room scenario. There are many ways that this sad but sometimes preventable outcome happens to well-meaning, Loving, and Caring Grandparents.

When I embarked on my CaringGrandparents.com site a decade or so ago I unwittingly fell into the sad and inexplicable stories of dysfunctional branches of extended families that Grandparents face all too often. I would receive comments on the Caring Grandparents Facebook page that would tear my heart out, throw it on the ground, and stomp on it. You may think that is hyperbole, but it is not. Take the following family story that is most typical of how this happens. Here is but one example.

Grandma Jill has three grown children. Her two boys got married quite young and each has two children. Her daughter is in college and engaged to be married soon.

Her relationship with her oldest son and his spouse who have been married for 7 years, is warm and close. Grandma Jill dotes on her 6-year-old Grandson and 3-year-old Granddaughter. Even though they live at a distance, Grandma Jill visits a couple of times a year. In the interim she has learned and consistently executed the best strategies of communicating with her long-distance Grandchildren as well as the parents. All signs point to these being Lasting Meaningful Connections between Grandma Jill and these two wonderful little bundles of Joy.

Her middle son, Jake, and his wife, Barbara, live nearby. They have been married for 5 years, and his marriage has disintegrated from being on rocky ground into an ugly divorce and custody battle.

Jill, being a Good Grandma, had practically raised Jake and Barbara's two young daughters. She babysat them both three days a week to help Jake and his wife out financially as well as to attempt to decrease the stress in their troubled marriage. The couple eventually separated, and her son moved back home with Grandma Jill. After a few court interventions, he managed to get visitation rights every other weekend.

On his weekend he brings the girls, Angie, and April, now 2 and 4, home to Grandma's house. Grandma is cautiously delighted that she gets to offer her heart to these two deserving beauties. But eventually, her son decides he is going to just go out with the boys. This cycle increases as does his drinking, even when he is with the girls. It becomes a volatile atmosphere that Grandma Jill tries to shield the girls from, but kids will be kids and this all gets back to Barbara.

Then, to add to the calamity, he falls behind on his Alimony/Child Support. Understandably, Mom Barbara is not happy with this situation and starts to refuse to allow the girls to come visit at all. Due to the arrears in Child support and the drinking, the courts agree with Mom.

This leaves Grandma sad and frustrated since Barbara is not about to let the kids visit Grandma since her son lives there. Grandma Jill has no control over any of this.

Another round of court battles ensues and the court, as it usually does, sides with the mother. Eventually, Jake loses visitation rights completely, and by extension, so does Grandma Jill. After the divorce, and Jake's loss of visitation rights, the ex-wife eventually remarries, and the new stepdad adopts the two girls.

Shocker but it is game over for Grandma Jill. Her years of Loving and caring for her Granddaughters' every need, the years of being their daytime child caregiver, the bond that only happens between a caring Grandmother and her Granddaughters is ripped away through no fault of her own. Grandma's phone calls aren't answered, her birthday cards and gifts for the girls are returned, and all contact and communications are stopped.

I would give a King's ransom to change this kind of outcome, but it is more prevalent than you think. Some of the parameters may change but the sad reality is that it does occur way too often.

Not all the situations are as clear and simple as the one involving Grandma Jill. There are many obstacles to a long and happy relationship with your Grandchildren. It is not a happy read, but it is instructive to learn, and even think about the wild and unusual circumstances that can cloud what should be a warm and wonderful Loving experience between Grandparent and Grandchild. It is my belief that knowing these unusual situations allows us to do even more by way of preemptive actions that better our chances of not falling victim to these extraordinary circumstances.

The reality is that some parents get incarcerated, become incapacitated, or even die. There is always the possibility of drug addiction, alcohol addiction, clinical depression, mental health issues, chronic unemployment, suicide, etc.

All of these will profoundly affect the family situation and your place in it as a Grandparent. If you see these kinds of things coming or are already there, your options are limited. Two of the possibilities are; first, you should align yourself with others going through the same kind of situation. It helps to share stories, strategies, and outcomes with like-minded Grandparents who are going through this as well. Second, is to organize any documentation of your involvement in your Grandchildren's lives. Don't rely on memory. Things like photos, videos, letters, your Treasure Trove pages, messages, etc. If it goes this far some state courts will consider the ongoing relationship when considering that alienation from the Grandparents may cause harm to the child.

Facebook is a good place to start looking for groups to learn from and gain some support. I will write about AGA (Alienated Grandparents Anonymous) later in this chapter.

The importance of knowing about all of these seemingly off-the-wall situations that occur much more often than you would think is that, in some cases, you will need to interject yourself into consideration by family law and/or court system in a timely manner to be even considered when things shake out from a legal standpoint. These are the kinds of circumstances that call for a Family Law attorney's advice. You will need to know that each state has its own independent and often diverse laws and guidelines when it comes to Grandparents' Rights.

Note: The laws in the state where the child resides are the ones that apply. One more quick point. Not to get too much into the legal weeds, but in some states, there are even stringent laws about who has legal standing to bring things like this to the court systems. This is why I advocate for the involvement of a Family Law Attorney if you must choose the legal route.

Please don't let all this legalese dissuade you from becoming part of a possible good outcome for your Grandchildren. Just become the best informed that you can and find the appropriate professional to guide you. This is way too important to all concerned to leave it up to others to resolve.

In many Family Law courts your intention and involvement help the court to see you as a possible good solution to an otherwise messy situation. I guess we are back to that "Never give up" advice.

While there are some things an alienated Grandparent can do, none of them are easy, very attractive, affordable, or even terribly effective. In my own case, I had, by divine guidance, stayed clear of the back and forth between my son and his first wife during the separation and divorce. I still carried on my relationship with my Granddaughter and treated her Mom with respect. I never talked with my granddaughter about what was going on with Mom and Dad. Somehow, I survived this tense and vulnerable time and maintained my connection to my now-grown Granddaughter. I am not sure where that wisdom came from, the word Grace comes to mind. I share it because it was a strategy that worked in my case. I still talk with and respect my ex-daughter-in-law. She knows I appreciate what a great job she has done raising such a beautiful soul. Disaster avoided.

Another scenario that all too frequently plays out is that two young people come together to form a family with all the dreams and aspirations that you and I have about a wonderful family with 2.5 kids, a white picket fence, a dog or two, and wedded bliss. Sound familiar?

Meet Jose and Maria; They start off in an apartment, which is the economically sound way to begin their lives together. Jose finds a decent-paying job with his uncle doing Vinyl Siding on new homes. He gets pretty good at his job. His uncle promotes him to foreman and gives him a nice raise. Maria, who had worked at the local Bagel shop a few days a week, is now with child.

In her 5th month, she starts to get some troublesome signs, and the Doctor tells her to go home and not to do anything that keeps her on her feet.

This obviously rules out the Bagel shop job, so she does as the Doctor says. She does it so well that she makes it almost full term, and to their joy, she delivers a precious little 6-pound 3-ounce girl. They named her Angelica. The baby is healthy, and their family life begins in earnest. They decided to try to buy a house in the coming year. They save and dream. When Angelica is almost one, Maria's mother, Rosa, comes to live close to them and offers to look after Angelica a few days a week. This allows Maria to find another job. This job is at the local hospital and pays a bit more than the Bagel shop did.

Things are looking up.

Within a few months, Maria finds out they will be a family of four in the new year. Fortunately, this pregnancy went a bit better. The entire family, including Grandma Rosa, starts talking about that house, but this time with an extra room for Grandma so she can watch the kids while Maria returns to work. Maria goes to full term, and little Jose is born healthy at 7 pounds 9 ounces. For the first 6 months after his birth Little Jose stays in a crib in Mom and Dad's room. It is time to start looking for that house. They are excited and eager to move on to the next stage of their life. The small apartment becomes just that. Small. Especially with an active 2-year-old. Dreams of a yard and swing set fill their heads as they look around for the perfect house.

Before they can find the appropriate home that they can afford Jose falls from a ladder at work. He survives but breaks his upper and lower leg in a couple of places. His uncle's company was too small to provide health insurance, but fortunately, they had purchased a bare-bones health policy that helped with some of the medical bills. It didn't wipe out all they had saved. The drawback was that with a bare bones policy there were no benefits that paid for missed work. They couldn't live on Maria's wages alone, so they had to dip into their savings just to get by.

Jose's leg took longer to heal than expected and he had considerable pain along the way. He may have reinjured it trying to get up and going too soon. More pain and, unfortunately, more pain medicine. At this point, there was considerable strain in the household. The pain and unproductiveness took a toll on Jose, and he spiraled deeper into himself and his pain pills.

Jose's parents lived out west and were undocumented, so their resources were sparse at best. They didn't know how bad things were. This is not something a family shouts from the rooftops.

As things got worse for Jose, Maria, thinking she was helping him, found a way to steal some meds from the hospital. This worked for a while, but eventually, she got caught, lost her job, and was facing charges and the potential of incarceration. Jose talked to his uncle, but his uncle could see that he was strung out and was unwilling to take the chance of him coming back to work. He refused Jose. With limited physical ability, Jose couldn't get a decent paying job. He also now needed his meds to function, even at a limited capacity. Things got worse and worse. Maria's mother even went to work to supplement her social security but that wasn't enough either.

With all this load, plus being unemployable, Maria began to show signs that she, too, had started using drugs. It didn't take long before the Child Welfare folks began to knock at their door. To protect their chosen lifestyle both Jose and Maria became combative and uncooperative.

In a panic, Grandma Rosa stepped up and offered to take in the children but was quickly disqualified for financial reasons. This is another case of a willing Grandparent, but the system prevails. When they finally did find out what was happening Jose's parents could not reveal themselves for fear of deportation. Even in this family with good intentions, things can happen to derail lives. I don't like telling these stories, but it should serve as a warning that it is best to really pay attention when it comes to our Grandkids.

There is an even darker side to Grandparent Alienation as well. While not as prevalent as being caught up in our own children's bad behavior, the idea of a sinister force of deliberate alienation is something to be aware of. I am not a psychologist or expert but the signs of this kind of Alienation eerily parallel the behaviors of abusive partners. Think along the lines of a spouse that has isolated your child from the family. One that tries to control every interaction for no obvious reason. There are those who seek to control every aspect of their partners and family behaviors.

Let's look at such a family. Your daughter starts hanging out with a guy that just makes everyone feel a bit edgy. While he is not overtly hostile, he doesn't make any effort to get to know or fit in with your family despite your attempts to include him. You begin to see signs of upheaval in their relationship. Your daughter becomes more and more isolated. She gets pregnant and they get married and move to another town several hours away. In short order, they have a second child. You are told about this but not invited to be a part of it. You do get a few visits but nothing like a warm and comfortable extended family gathering. You begin to feel a distance being opened between you and your daughter as well as the Grandchildren. This is not the same child you once had a close relationship with, but you keep trying to build bridges. It seems that nothing you do forges a closer bond with any of the family. Truth be known, while unspoken, you can see it in the eyes of your daughter and now your somewhat older Grandchildren. Despite your daughter's and grandchildren's efforts to hide it, it still looks like despair and fear.

Regardless of your efforts, you feel every move you and/or the family make is under the watchful eye and control of the son-in-law. There seems to be an implied threat to the relationship you have with your Grandkids, and your daughter is not very helpful when it comes to how and when you interact with the Grandchildren. Over time, the isolation and control take a turn towards terms and demands of you as Grandparents. If you want to see the Grandkids, then you will have to do this or that.

This actually occurs and it surfaces in some of the many Grandparenting Groups around the United States as well as abroad. If this is even remotely ringing a bell, then I suggest one important resource that zeroes in specifically on this kind of situation. The best resource I have come across for troubled Grandparents is the "AGA". Alienated Grandparents Anonymous. Visit https://alienatedgrandparentsanonymous.com for

Newsletter, Professionals, Success Stories, Support Groups, etc. There are many other resources, but AGA seems to do it best. The one overriding message is taken from Winston Churchill during the second World War; "Never, never, never give up."

I proffer two suggestions that I have heard to be the most effective among the sparse options.

In the Never-Give-Up category.

One completely cut off Grandma came up with the idea of a Memory Kit, which consists of things like those returned birthday cards and letters, as well as mementos that she held sacred about each Grandchild, etc. This becomes Golden if and when your Grandchild grows up and comes looking for more of that Grandma or Grandpa Love. Just imagine the incredible boost for that child to know that through the years they were in your heart all along. Good idea. Actually, it's a Great idea.

Most Grandmothers still have a box of letters, some sent and returned, and some just written and put in a drawer over the years. These seem to be as valuable to the writer as they are if the Grandchild shows up after they turn 18 and return for more Love.

I am a fan of the Ancestry stories that reunite parents after many years. There are also a lot of heartwarming stories of grown children trying to find and reconnect with long lost Grandparents that had Loved and cared for them when they were small.

In the keep Hope alive category.

A suggestion is to cherish and celebrate any other Grandchildren you do get to stay connected to. Learn, learn, and learn all you can from other Alienated

Grandparents and vow to not make some of the mistakes they share about how they came to be in this large and growing group of devastated Grandparents. Continue your Journey with each and all of them and share your Gratitude with all who will hear.

Finally, when it comes to prevention of alienation there are some best practices for you to avoid the pitfalls and silent undercurrents of resentment that sometimes happen without us even knowing. The Journey from Good to Great Grandparenting is not necessarily paved with good intentions, but the path is made smoother and more possible with Best Practices.

The first, foremost, and sometimes hard to get used to, is to truly partner with the parents of your Grandchildren.

In the case where you are partnering with your own child, you must, for the benefit of all concerned, find a way to bury any remaining hatchets, and annihilate your "I'm still in charge" EGO. Make it a point to stifle the need to instruct your child on the best way to raise their child.

Keep your metaphorical roll of Duct Tape handy. Once again be reminded, this is THEIR child.

Bond with your Daughter-in-law or Son-in-law. Get to know them and treat them with even more respect than they deserve. As the Bible says in both the Old and New Testament, Genesis 2-24, Mathew 19 5-6, and Ephesians 5-31, "For this reason a man will leave his father and mother and be united to his wife, and the two will become one flesh." This must be pretty important to span those many years and warrant three mentions. Just sayin'. You don't have to like it, but your Grandparenting will go soooooo much better if you do.

Ask, ask, ask the new parents to be, just how they would like this whole birthing thing to go. Be especially tuned into the wishes of the mother of this new miracle about to be born. If you are the maternal Grandparents your status is totally different than if you are the paternal Grandparents. This successful Grandparenting is a marathon, not a sprint or a photo op.

Be thoughtful in your gift giving, especially early on. This is not a competition between Grandparents. Just some more food for thoughtfulness.

Grow in knowledge about your Grandchild as they themselves grow. This is the secret sauce of creating a Lasting Meaningful Relationship with each Grandchild.

Consult the parents early and often. The most beautiful song is when the parents and you sing from the same hymnal and sing the same song, in harmony.

You may think it is cute to spoil your Grandkids. It is probably not cute nor is it productive. Pay close attention to what is going on with your Grandchildren both online and off.

Teach your Grandchildren about your Gratitude Journal. A great place to start is with what is really wonderful about their parents.

Chapter 10

GREAT AND GRAND HEROES

> "Heroes are ordinary people who make themselves extraordinary."
>
> Gerard Way

This chapter is written for the many, now almost 3 million, Grandparents who were "given" an opportunity to step up and become Great and Grand heroes. These are the folks caught in the crosshairs of circumstances not of their own making that change their lives in fundamental ways. They are each the last best hope for these vulnerable children. These Grandparents deal each day with all kinds of trauma in addition to their own ambivalent feelings about their station at this time in their own lives. Great they are, Heroes each and every one of them are.

Two of those 3 million just happen to be my friends of over 50 years. Their first daughter Loretta, who is still like a daughter to me, had her first baby in her teens. Ill-equipped to take proper care of her daughter on her own, they both stayed with Grandma Pam and Grandpa Sam.

I still remember my first time meeting my new quasi-Granddaughter. When I came into the house Grandma Pam was holding baby Kylie. Grandma proudly stood up to present this beautiful bundle to me. She handed her off to me, and I knew enough to support her 4-day-old head as I gently put her up onto my shoulder. My thanks for being such a considerate quasi-Grandpa was that Kylie peed all over my shirt. "Well, howdy to you too little one!" So, I did the only thing I could do, I nicknamed her Puddle.

I told this story at Grandpa Sam's funeral and the friends and family then understood why I had called this now grown woman with her own beautiful family Puddle her entire life.

Grandma and Grandpa never wavered in their Love for Kylie. From her first breath until now, some 4 decades later, Puddle knew she was significant, Loved, and cared for. They raised her up to be a wonderful young Lady. She and her husband now look after her Grandma and have raised a wonderful family of their own.

As we grow older, we make plans to enjoy the fruits of our labor and retire, visit with all the Grandkids, maybe travel, and do the things we have always wanted to do. Nothing can get in the way of our plans, or can it? "BAM, Crunch, Zip, Boom and Kerplunk, Life Happens!

One such Grandmother shared this story. Anna, affectionately known as MeeMaw, had retired early to spend as much time with her preteen Grandchildren as possible. Her husband, known as Grandpa Ben, had 7 years left before retirement. They saved and planned and saved some more. They spent many evenings plotting their trip across the country in a not-yet-purchased RV with stops at all the tourist attractions they couldn't afford while raising their own family, which included an older daughter and her little brother. With the family finally grown up and out on their own, it was time to dream a little. This trip included a stop at their son's house to see them and their 10 and 12-year-old boys out west.

Before Ben's retirement, their oldest daughter, Sarah, had made some bad choices and got hooked on drugs. Her husband, Billy, was probably the source. Fortunately, Meemaw and Grandpa Ben had just visited them to find some pretty deplorable conditions in the home that their Grandson, Jimmy, was living in. He wasn't eating properly, his clothes were disheveled, and he had been missing school a lot. Alarmed at all of this they returned home and immediately started the process of saving their Grandson.

Sarah became indefensibly resistant to the idea of her son Jimmy coming to live with his Grandpa Ben and Meemaw. The only alternative was an expensive court battle that drained some of their retirement savings. It didn't take long for the courts to understand the severity of the situation and they awarded temporary Guardianship to the Grandparents. As if this wasn't bad enough, to add insult to injury, Billy's parents were in denial and consequently of no help at all.

This accomplished the first step for the rescue of Jimmy, but the courts moved very slowly and cautiously. This may not make sense to you as Caring Grandparents, but the court will, in a heartbeat, award Jimmy back to his Mom, if she even acts like she is going to do better. There doesn't have to be any proof; she just says the word; and the courts generally go along with the birth mother. The good and bad news in this case is that Child Protective Services found the living conditions in the apartment of Sarah and Billy were nasty at best. The other contributing factor was the many "friends" of Billy and Sarah who were showing up at their door at all hours of the day and night.

This did help Anna and Ben to finally get full custody, but not until a considerable amount of their retirement savings had been transferred to the lawyer's bank accounts. Now you get an idea why I term these Grandparents heroes.

After the heart-crushing disappointment of losing a daughter to drugs and having their retirement derailed by circumstances not of their own doing, Meemaw and Grandpa Ben awakened the day after the court awarded them full custody of their grandson, to their new reality. They had to begin a new life, which included a deferred retirement and the responsibility of raising an 11-year-old boy, (probably saving their grandson's life in the process.) All three were embarking upon a life they did not choose for themselves, I might add, but a new and different life all the same.

According to the US census there are over 2.7 million Grandparents that are spending their Retirement time as the responsible people for their Grandchildren. About half of these are 60 or over. In addition, there are another 5 million Grandparents living with Grandchildren in their home that are under the age of 18.

This is something we can't close our eyes to and hope it goes away. The reasons for this societal dilemma matter and go way beyond the scope of this book; however, one extremely important consideration is the fallout. This goes beyond Good Samaritan stuff. These Grandparents are rescuers of the highest order. I don't use the term Hero lightly.

As an example of heroic folks, take my friend Jim. He is exceptional on several levels. Jim lost his son James at an early age after a brief illness. His son, James and James' wife Brenda had two boys 2 years apart. Jim's widowed daughter-in-law fell into the double role of both Mom and Dad fairly naturally, but not without the support of both sides of the family and a caring community. Two years after their loss of a father, the boy's mother, Brenda, was tragically killed by a drunk driver in an auto accident.

While battling her own health issues, Brenda's Mom Grammy, stepped up to raise the boys, now 4 and 6 years old. Grammy Linda had a lot of help from both sides of the family and her community, as well. But it wasn't long after this second tragedy that Grammy got too sick to care for the boys.

After Jim consulted with his new wife, Jenny, the pair agreed to take the boys into their home and raise them. This situation was extremely unusual in that very seldom does the paternal Grandfather become the Guardian, and on top of that, his new wife suddenly found herself thrust into a very unexpected situation.

In short order, they adopted the boys. Consider for a moment this detour in Jim and Jenny's plans of starting a new life together. Absolutely no one sits down and plots this radical of a change of plans. To their credit, they each decided to make this work and set the course to parent these boys. Some 15 years later, I am happy to report the boys are now 19 and 21 years old, and thanks to a Loving home, they turned out to be Loving and Lovable, fine young men. It is because of people like Jim and his then-new bride, Jenny, that these boys have been given a framework of stability and Love in which to thrive.

Very few families could have survived these triple tragedies. Thank God for willing family members, especially Jim's new bride Jenny. The boys affectionately call her Mom which is a testament to her stepping up all these years as well. Would anyone begrudge Jim and Jenny the title of Grand Hero?

This story speaks to willing family members. This is not always the case. In too many cases the Grandparents are the last resort. Too many of these families don't have the wherewithal to take on more hungry mouths and the sole responsibility for their Grandchildren yet they are thrust into this role. As I concluded in the first paragraph, Life Happens. When it does, the entire world of these Grandparents is suddenly turned on its head, but they usually do the best they can.

This story brings to mind a memory of me reading a cool little book to my own kids when they were small. The book is "Hope for the Flowers" by Trina Paulus. Because of all of the Grand Heroes who have become this HOPE, these flowers are able to grow and bloom. If you are a Grand Hero, please take a bow and accept my admiration for what you do.

In present times, over a million Grandparents must deal with the consequences of drug addiction, incarceration, or both. I can't even imagine the sadness that accompanies the disappointment of watching your own children sink deeper and deeper into the abyss of addiction and your need to redirect your own life on behalf of your Grandchildren. The struggles are huge. Even if they are okay with setting aside their own hopes and dreams once they decide to accept the responsibility of more mouths to feed, minds to educate, and bodies to clothe. In most of these cases, there has already been unimaginable emotional damage to the Grandkids before their rescue.

Moreover, there are practical and/or legal barriers, simple things like picking up the kids from school without parental permission when the parents are checked out and absent. Then there is the challenge of medical care, which most times requires involving the glacially slow, overcrowded, and expensive judicial system. Add to these everyday roadblocks the fact that the Grandparents must sit on the edge of that child's bed each night and try to explain why Mommy and Daddy aren't home to tuck them in. Yes, it breaks my heart also.

You will remember from the story of Anna and Ben that if the parents get sober for just a little while the courts will give the kids back to the parents. Grandma and Grandpa may as well mark their calendar because within a month or so, once again, they will have to go re-rescue the Grandkids, with now additional emotional and sometimes physical damage. This happens way too often and, in most cases, repeatedly.

When I was researching my books on Grandparents Rights, I was sharing what I was up to with a longtime friend Bill. He was helping me with the materials for a bath remodel job at my local supply house. That normally 20-minute process led to coffee and many hours of him sharing his story.

This is an example of how quickly Grandparents' Hopes and Dreams can be hijacked.

Bill and his wife Judy came home early one evening to a driveway and front yard surrounded by crime tape and police cars. When they approached one of the officers and identified themselves as the homeowners, they were told they couldn't go inside. But this is our home and those are our Grandchildren and our Daughter. The officer said their daughter was okay, but their Grandson was injured and on his way to the hospital. You must wait until we sort this out.

Let me introduce you to this 50-something couple. Bill and Judy owned and operated a small bath remodeling company for a few years together. They lovingly raised a son and daughter during this time. As the economy contracted, their income also contracted, and it was decided that Judy would get another job, so she went to work for a local Interior Designer in town. As things got a bit worse, Bill went to work for his local Plumbing Supply house, helping with their bath redesign clients. That is where I got to know him when he was helping me with a project I was working on.

We became friends and had many discussions about our families. He and Judy were two hard-working, responsible, Loving folks raising a family and living in a nice home. As time went on their oldest child, Janet, married and had two children of her own. As time passed, her marriage was on again, off again so, for stability, Janet and the kids moved back home with her parents. Not ideal but Bill and Judy made the best of the situation and, truthfully, kind of liked being around their now 5- and 2-year-old Grandkids.

As the months went by and the children's father became less stable and more volatile, Bill and Judy had to lay down the law. He could visit his children but not at their home. This caused a ruckus. Then, several weeks after these new arrangements were instituted, Janet's estranged husband came, broke into the home and shot at her. He missed her but some of the shrapnel injured their 2-year-old son. Fortunately, he missed Janet but it injured Jacob. They arrested the dad.

This is what Bill and Judy had come home to.

Now, a few years later, I am happy to report that Jacob has healed from the physical wounds. Naturally, there are deep and lasting psychological wounds to everyone in the family, especially Jacob.

To add to the enormous burden of all of this, their daughter isn't handling it well, so Bill and Judy were thrust into the role of raising their two Grandchildren. As Grandparents, they have to endure many court procedures and enormous expenses just to secure some stability for these two young children.

As you might imagine, the father is uncooperative, so the proceedings drag out. As a means to gain custody and parental rights, Bill and Judy are forced to give some concessions which include the father having supervised visits with the kids at a psychologist's office.

To quote my first book, "There are times when we find Logic and Law to be strange bedfellows." I can't begin to fathom the pain this causes everyone in the family. Family Law, especially when it comes to parents' rights, is something of a mystery, but the kid's survival and stability must come first. God Bless Bill and Judy!

Bill reports that Jacob is adjusting remarkably well, especially thanks to a chance encounter in their faith community that led to a connection with the right folks. These specialized resources that deal with survivors of this kind of trauma are rare and expensive and the healing process is long and challenging. Their faith community has been a savior to their financial survival as a family. Bill and Judy are soldiering on, and things are a bit better but not great with their daughter. I would have to place them in the Great Grandparent category with a Grand Hero badge. I hope there is a special place for them in Heaven.

One more sad statistic is that about one-third of the 2.7 million Grandparent households that are raising their Grandkids are below the poverty line, which is less than $25,000.00 annually for a family of three. These statistics touch all racial and ethnic lines. Just like the drug addiction issue, this is an equal misery crisis for these folks and their Grandchildren, both economically and emotionally. The sad thing is that most times when Grandparents become parents again, it is for more than one Grandchild. For those in the bottom one third economically it presents a further challenge. At that level, food insecurity is added to the already tremendous burden of their retirement life. Unlike the first story in this chapter, these folks don't have a retirement savings account to dig into.

This chapter started with the quote from Gerald Way; "Heroes are ordinary people who make themselves extraordinary". I don't think the term Hero is hyperbole when it comes to those willing to put their lives on hold to rescue these vulnerable souls in a time of crisis. The good news is that these Heroes don't have to go it alone. There are more and more programs, agencies, and general support available now than at any time before.

Family Therapy. Family therapy can help individuals and families cope with their feelings about their family situation, resolve problems, and improve the quality of their relationships. Family therapists are specially trained to understand the complicated feelings and relationships experienced by grandparents and their grandchildren. If you feel that your family could benefit from family therapy, seek a therapist who has experience working with grandparents raising grandchildren.

Support Groups. Many communities offer support groups for grandparents raising grandchildren. Although most of these support groups are for grandparents, some groups are also available for grandchildren. Support groups provide participants with an opportunity to talk about their experiences and feelings in a safe, supportive environment. Participants can also gain information about local resources, learn from one another, and meet people dealing with similar issues.

Good support groups allow time for personal sharing, but also take a positive outlook, structure sharing time, connect participants to sources of support, and help participants to set and reach goals. To find a support group near you, visit the websites of the organizations listed under "Resources" or contact a trusted professional in your area. Online support communities are also available, though you would want to carefully assess their quality.

Other Services. Grandparents raising grandchildren may be eligible for a variety of other services and support including financial assistance, food and nutrition programs, free or low-cost medical care, respite care, and housing assistance, among others. To learn more about these services, consult the "Resources" listed below or ask a trusted professional such as a caseworker, clergy, school counselor, or health care provider.

Chapter 11

YOUR GRANDPARENTING LEGACY

> "What impact are you making, not only today, but for eternity? What impact are you making to leave a legacy?"
>
> Kirk Cousins

> "The one thing I need to leave behind is good memories".
>
> Michael Landon
> Little House on the Prairie

One way to define your Grandparenting Legacy is this; It is the story that will be told about you. It will have a lot to do with how you made them feel when you connected with them. It is your gift to your Grandchildren. It is a story of the value that you delivered to your Grandchildren.

Wow, that is almost a scary thought. Pondering your Legacy is all the more reason to maximize this Journey. Leave no stone unturned.

Paradoxically, legacy is all about us, yet it is really all about your contribution to others. It is the impression you leave on others that outlasts you. If you choose to become Great at this Grandparenting Journey, you will leave a long-lasting and powerful legacy. The more you get to know and Love each of your Grandchildren, the more you contribute to their sense of significance, their sense of you being present to them. The more you listen to them, the greater your legacy.

As Grandparents, we have this vast body of earned wisdom we wish to impart to our Grandkids, and that is admirable. The facts point to those one-on-one encounters, those otherwise unremarkable events that they will carry with them. It is how you make each child feel about themselves when they are with you that counts the most. If you are failing to stay connected with them it is wasted wisdom.

When I was a Youth Minister, the kids I was working with were entering and/or already in the dating phase of their lives. To set the stage, I was more of a question asker than a preacher type of Youth leader. One of the questions I asked, especially of the young ladies, was "How do you feel about yourself when you are with this person?" Not so much about how you feel about them, but trusting your gut, how you feel about you.

This method of doling out advice, if you can even call it that, was most effective. If you think about it, it carries over to almost every meaningful decision in our lives. We are given an inner compass, and we seem to do pretty well when we trust it and follow it.

In a lightning-fast-moving world we can stand as pillars of unconditional love and offer a sense of stability and timelessness to our family by example. This is especially true in a world that often seems preoccupied with the fleeting moments of today. It is essential for us to reflect on our enduring Legacy as Grandparents. Many talk about leaving their footprints in the sand, but those go away with the tides. I like to think of taking this intentional Grandparenting Journey as footprints in the cement walk with our initials and the date right beside them.

Will we leave a trail of the power of love, resilience, and tradition? Have we done all we can to convey a message of cherished moments with each Grandchild? Will we be remembered for helping them shape their values and/or guiding them on the path they choose as their way in the world? Will we be remembered for lifting them up through our actions and words, encouraging them at every step? I, for one, choose to be the best "Good Seer and Good Sayer' that I can be.

Just what will they remember when they think back on their time with us? It is our script to write any way we wish. It is our play to act out to our Grandchildren as the audience. The responsibility is great but the outcome we can choose will be even better. This is our chance to impart our wisdom through who we are, rather than just what we say.

This is a good spot for you to return to the answers you gave in Chapter One about your vision of yourself as a Grandparent as well as the pages of information, Hopes, and Dreams for each of your Grandchildren.

To add to the importance of this Chapter, I remind you that now your Legacy is in your hands; after you are gone, it is in the hands of your Grandchildren. I am pretty sure they will remember how you made them feel significant rather than the fact that you often dribbled spaghetti sauce on your shirt or fell asleep in your easy chair almost every night when you visited them.

When it comes to the physical Legacy of personal items you leave, it is my hope that you will apply the same thoughtfulness that you do when you meet them where they are. When it comes to finances, my Mom left each Grandchild an equal percentage of her money. It wasn't that much, but it impacted each one of them with the thought that their Grandma thought of them as important.

The equal distribution is the common advice given by Estate Attorneys. This is something that you can alter to suit your family, but I bet whatever you decide about your money will pale in comparison to the intangibles that will comprise the story your Grandchildren will tell about you. Keep in mind that people quickly forget what you say but long remember how you made them feel.

Another area of Legacy is the ancestry from whence they came. Grandchildren are fascinated with the stories of their ancestors. There are studies which confirm that children and Grandchildren who have a sense of the roots of their family are more inclined to have a secure feeling of belonging.

In the case of our family, my Little Sister Salle and I collaborated to find and get prints of our Taft Family Tree. In our case we have an interesting guy on our family tree. We found that William Howard Taft, the 27th President of the United States is our 5th cousin. Even more interesting is that I have had the opportunity to tell my children and Grandchildren about the person he was, which overshadows the politician he was. As a politician he was, by the nature of the beast, controversial. The overarching characteristic that he brought to our family is his Fairness and Honesty as a Judge and later Chief Justice of the Supreme Court. This and many stories of our family tree make for great reinforcement of the strength of character he has passed down through the family. Think, Good Seer and Good Sayer.

I can reinforce this family trait by the story of Robert Taft Sr. who was the first Taft to come to this country in the late 1670s. Robert and his wife Sarah set up a homestead in Mendon Mass. (now called Uxbridge). He happened to be a surveyor as were his sons after him. Surveyors of that era were known to be some of the most trusted professionals. There still stands a bridge in Uxbridge, known as the bridge the Tafts built. So as not to make a long story longer I share this because it sparked interest in all my children and Grandchildren. My point is that it is a surefire way to drive home the point of Honesty and Integrity in our family's bloodline as well as a sense of belonging, all wrapped up in an interesting story.

No matter the history I bet you can find some interesting ancestors and share them with your Grandkids.

One oft' forgotten method of passing down family stories was what, in medieval times, was called an Ethical Will. Some called it a Spirit Will. This was normally in addition to a Real Property Will. Most recently they show up in the Jewish tradition. The first mentions I found were Genesis 49:1-33. "Jacob", Deuteronomy 32: 46 & 47. "Moses" and Mathew: 5 "Jesus". These types of (Wishes Wills) also showed up in Germany, France, and Spain, in the 11th and 12 centuries.

I mention that to let you know that being intentional about your Grandparent Legacy puts you in some mighty fine company. You have worked really hard for this thing we call wisdom; I think it is natural to want to pass it on to our little ones. Before I leave this subject let me leave you with a Nugget of Wisdom that I read; "Kindness is more important than wisdom, and the recognition of this is the beginning of Wisdom." This quote by Dr. Theodore Isaac Rubin takes wisdom to the next level.

My hope is that you will give a tremendous amount of thought about your Grandparent Legacy. Whatever vehicle you create to pass along your story is valid for you. When it comes to your Legacy, I like to harken back to those big family meals surrounding Thanksgiving and listen to the table talk. That seems to be the best incubator for what you leave behind to help others do the same.

Chapter 12

WHAT ABOUT SOCIAL MEDIA?
Parts A, B, & C

"People crave comfort, people crave connection, people crave community."

Marianne Williamson

These platforms offer us, as grandparents, an insight into the world of our Grandchildren that has never before existed. It is like being a fly on the wall in their everyday lives. Look, Listen and Learn.

Caveat: Some of you reading this are far ahead of the rest of us. Forgive me but I am being basic, especially in part A, to help those who choose to learn and are trying to catch up with their Grandkids.

You can learn more about your Grandchildren's world by observing where they spend their time and energy. This is an interesting and informative window into their world. Just ask them to help you and they will be glad to tell you. The good news is that most of the platforms they are on can be observed without signing up for them. I have tried to facilitate that for you in this chapter.

Confession time again. I initially did my research on some of these platforms in the strict observation mode, as listed below. My Loving 18-year-old Granddaughter offered to help me sign up for a few of the sites over the holidays. I did and she showed me how to navigate around. It is fascinating and instructive. Then I had to suffer the ribbing by all three of my Grandkids and my own kids about being addicted to this newfangled toy I had found. All kidding aside, those algorithms are definitely designed to suck you in and keep you engaged. Good News, I am back home and still in recovery from my newfound addiction. In all seriousness, I do have a more visceral understanding of how these things work.

The reason I am separating this chapter into General, part B, and Part C is because there is so much hoopla about the internet, Social Media, etc. My purpose is to be inclusive of where each Grandparent is when it comes to their knowledge and participation in this thing known as Social Media. This is an important chapter and can better identify our possible contributions as Grandparents when it comes, not only to Social Media but to the world our young people are immersed in. The first part will deal with the overarching stuff, a sort of Dos and Don't that are suggested by many experienced leaders when it comes to kids and the Internet. Part A has more to do with how to use Social Media in a way that enhances our connection and interaction with our Grandchildren without getting in the way of the groups of friends that they share those platforms with. Part B is addressed to those who have taken the plunge and become active on some of these platforms. The adventurous Grandparents can offer deeper insights to those of us who are just dipping our toes in the water at this time. Part C has to do with our as well as our Grandchildren's safety and responsible use of this wild west technology they spend significant time on.

Social Media in general.

With everyone bad-mouthing Social Media, one would think that I follow the herd on this one. Au contraire! I happen to think there are many good things about Social Media. I recognize the opportunity for us as Grandparents to get a look inside the world our Grandkids inhabit each day. I just happen to believe that we as adults can put up some guardrails and help our Grandkids better navigate this inevitable technology. This is the challenge, our Grandchildren are on many Social Media platforms, some of which we have never heard of. While this is not quite like the blind leading the blind, I will take you to where you can become a bit more familiar, and hopefully more comfortable with some of it that is very familiar and even natural for your Grandkids. I realize some of you may be way ahead of the rest of us when it comes to this area of your Grandchildren's life, but it may be useful to refresh your memory a bit. My point of view in this book is the result of continually consulting my three teen Grandchildren and my one 30-something Grandson. The experts in this area provide us with three major caveats to Social Media when it comes to those we love. First and foremost is that the parents and Grandparents be familiar with all the places our Grandchildren spend their time when they are on Social Media.

Second is that we work with the parents to erect appropriate guardrails when it comes to the safety and protection of our Grandkids. And third is to ask your Grandchildren when and where, or even if, they want you to interact with them on the platforms they are on. This last one is a tough call but there are ways this can be done to enhance our connections to them while not embarrassing them. More to come on this point.

Let's take these one at a time. The biggest beast in the room is Facebook. This is the one platform that many Grandparents are familiar with and probably use the most. As for this one, you will have to consult with both parents and Grandkids about what you post. There are safety concerns when you mention things like what school they go to, etc. My purpose is not to make you paranoid but rather to encourage you to be considerate. Many young folks are moving away from Facebook and/or don't check it much, others are very active and embrace you interacting with them in this space. My admonition is to check in with them and their parents to get some guidance here. What we think is cute they may not think of in the same way. Just checking in with them will usually cover your bases.

One example is that, on Facebook, I will only comment on the stuff their parents put up there. The "Like" feature lets them know you are interested in what they are up to, and it is kind of innocuous. I personally use Messenger in most of my interactions on Facebook. I do have a grown Grandson who likes to think he is "cute" on his page. In his case, I only respond to affirming and thoughtful posts. His Mom and I have a plan to only affirm the better posts. The good news is that he has gotten the message. It is still a work in progress, but I have noticed an uptick in more thoughtful posts coming from him. I think the term positive reinforcement applies here.

I use Twitter (now called X) to send what I call Electronic Hugs as well as positive and supportive messages to them a few times a week. Short, sweet, and to the point, lets them know I am thinking about them. I get some fun and interesting comments back from them. (If they don't answer right away or even ever, it is OK) Not everyone has to answer every ring or ding on their phone. I recognize that they have very active lives, so I don't obsess over it. I also find that for myself.

Snapchat and Instagram seem to rank high with my Grandchildren. My youngest Grandchild is 15 years old. I must admit that I came to the idea of learning these platforms kicking and screaming, but I do know the power of meeting them where they are, and they are on these platforms. Even with my reluctance I do understand that this is one of those investments in them. As often happens, when you plow new ground, you will find new things. I have learned so much about their world and this only enhances my bonds with each and every one of my Grandchildren. It is up to you to find your own footing on these. I have late teen Granddaughters and while I may observe, I don't feel it is my place to be commenting to their friends about them. If invited I may affirm something but I consider this their territory and so I mostly observe and learn.

One afternoon recently I spent about a half hour going through Instagram videos with my 15-year-old Grandson. It was interesting and instructive to hear what he had to say about each video. Some he wanted me to send to his friends, some he wanted to send to his Mom, etc. I was surprised to find out he had an interest in astronomy. He kept having me drill down on some astronomy videos. It is not quite like reading a book together, but it is eye opening. I will repeat, this new technology allows us Grandparents to have a window into their world that never existed before. It is worth learning how to best use this stuff to enhance your understanding of your grandkids.

Social Media is a double-edged sword for many reasons. As I stated in Chapter 3 about Lasting Meaningful Connections. I have no inclination nor is it appropriate for Grandpa Neil to be all up in my Granddaughters Instagram stuff where she likes to share with her friends. That is her space and as Loving as she is she would probably not say anything, but I intuitively know that is not appropriate. I guess we are back to basics. This is not about me being a cool Grandpa, it is about respecting her space. I do, however, let them know that I am paying attention to these platforms as well, and if I find inappropriate or threatening stuff having to do with them, they know I will let their parents know.

Speaking of Guardrails. I think it only fair that we consider a few of our own Do's and Don'ts when it comes to how we present on these Social Media Networking Platforms. On the spectrum from just observing to engaging on some or all of these sites here are some thoughts that may help. We have all heard about the Grandparent who thought it was "cute" to show one of the Grandkids in a, once funny, but now that they have grown up a bit embarrassing picture or story. My mantra is "when in doubt, leave it out". I will however share a video or comment that I think will add value to them when I see it, but always in messenger It can be a tool for good.

Ask, ask, ask. This is a good guiding principle when it comes to posting anything anywhere on Social Media. If it is something that is congratulatory and or affirming, say on Facebook, about some accomplishment they or their parents have posted, go for it. If you have any doubts just ask their parents first. I text my Grandkids and ask them to call me at their convenience. When they do, I just ask them if I would be overstepping if I, say wished their friends that I have met, a Happy Birthday, or congratulations on an accomplishment. When in doubt I just skip it. I try to find a balance that is short of being in their stuff and sufficient to let them know I am paying attention and I care deeply about them and what is going on with them. So far so good.

When I decided to include this chapter in this book, I polled my Grandkids and several sets of parents and Grandparents. My decision to include this is born out of the wide diversity of reactions from talking with these folks. The more I broadened my research the more varied the responses became. I then researched the newly minted experts on the subject. I say newly minted because this is new territory for all of us.

You will be amazed at how many Grandparents are on some of these platforms. If you are curious just enter Grandparenting into the search function on any of the platforms and you will get an eye-opening idea of just how many entries exist from and about Grandparents.

I am amazed at how comfortable my Grandchildren are with Social Media. My approach is to have them teach me about the various sites they use. This not only helps me understand the technology, but it spurs a conversation about the whys and wherefores of each platform. It also opens the conversation about how they want me to communicate with them. The added bonus is that it equates to meeting them exactly where they are.

As I stated earlier, many young people are moving away from Facebook. If your Grandchildren are still on that platform be sure to check with them before you comment on their public page. To be sure I won't embarrass them I use Messenger to ask them if what I am about to respond with is OK. If I find a video on Facebook that I think they may like I send it in Messenger so they can filter it if they wish.

Admittedly there is a flip side to the good. This is all the more reason to include the parents in this discussion. If our Grandkids hear the same out of our mouths about their use and boundaries on Social Media, it will only reinforce what they have already been told at home.

There are many effective ways to steer our Grandkids away from danger. I am a firm believer that the most destructive and least effective method of keeping them safe online is to use shame. I think when parents and Grandparents use shaming as a technique it is because they aren't willing to put in the work of trying alternative and more effective methods. I have offered a sure-fire way to steer our Grandkids by using "Good Seeing and Good Saying" Some authority figures resort to "Bad Seeing and Shaming" Please, please, don't take the easy way out. This is a good place to interject my emphatic and profound desire to rid this society of the use of shame.

I must admit that I may have resorted to this easy-way-out method of parenting from time to time. For this I apologize profusely to my children. I Love the way Brene Brown, the author of a great book called "Daring Greatly" defines Shame as the Swamp of the Soul. That brings to mind a nasty place to be. By the way, the title of her book, "Daring Greatly" came from a quote from Theodore Roosevelt's poem "the Arena" that has everything to do with defying shame as a weapon. It has everything to do with taking the road less traveled. It has everything to do with affirming the courage to try. You have probably heard it but this time it may serve you and your Grandkids to sit with it for a while.

"It is not the critic who counts; not the man who points out how the strong man stumbles, or where the doer of deeds could have done them better. The credit belongs to the man who is actually in the arena, whose face is marred by dust and sweat and blood; who strives valiantly; who errs, who comes short again and again, because there is no effort without error and shortcoming; but who does actually strive to do the deeds; who knows great enthusiasms, the great devotions; who spends himself in a worthy cause; who at the best knows in the end the triumph of high achievement, and who at the worst, if he fails, at least fails while daring greatly, so that his place shall never be with those cold and timid souls who neither know victory nor defeat."

- Theodore Roosevelt

The truth is that one misplaced comment from a significant person at the wrong time can trigger enough shame to prevent them from ever entering "The Arena". This is the exact opposite of what I am trying to do for and with my Grandchildren, every day of their lives.

Let me tell you a business story that will illustrate the profound power of the triggers that shame can cause.

When I was doing some Real Estate investing in Charlotte, North Carolina I ran across a property that was in the path of progress and was occupied by a tenant. The house was passed down to the siblings by their last living parent. The current owner and his then wife had lived there about 10 years prior to me meeting him. He had borrowed some money against that house to buy out the rest of his siblings. When things went south with his marriage, his wife moved out, so he got an apartment and leased out the house. Her not being there put him in a financial bind. The property, to be generous, had some challenges.

Fast forward a couple of years and he remarried. The one stipulation the new wife had was that she had no interest in living in the same house he and his previous wife had lived in. I found all this out as I sat with them one evening in an effort to see if they were willing to sell. The circumstances played out that he owed considerably more than it was worth in its present condition. This hampered the new couple from moving forward in their new life together since this debt now reflected on her credit as his wife. The solution that I could offer was to get the deed and their permission to negotiate with the lender to try for what is called a short sale. That is where the lender realizes that some part of recovery of the note is better than none. My Promise to the newlywed couple was that I would stipulate that the lender had to release them from any shortfall to the collateral if I bought the property. Based on the prospect that they would get out from under this debt they agreed and signed all the appropriate documents.

I then contacted the lender and faxed (I know, but this was in 1998) the needed paperwork to the lender. They sent me back the name and number of who I needed to contact within their company to negotiate the short sale. I contacted this gentleman. I remember his first name was Jeb. We talked for a few minutes, and he basically said that they were not interested in taking less for the property than what was on the note. I didn't get excited, I merely asked two questions that I already knew the answers to. I first asked if there had been an appraisal when they did the loan. He said he wasn't sure. Since he was required to send me the closing documents, I knew there had not been one. My next question was, had they inspected the property since they made the loan. Again, said he didn't know, but the answer according to the present owner was also no. Armed with this info I used what is known in negotiation tactics as the shout back. I asked Jeb, "Did your company loan the present owner $48,500.00 on this property?" He looked at his documents and said yes. I raised my voice some and said, "Shame on You"! Silence _____ on both ends of the conversation. I waited and waited. He began to stutter, stammer, and get all flustered.

I only used information that we both knew to be true. I didn't disparage Jeb as a person. He did not personally make this loan. The only thing I did was to invoke shame and it triggered him so badly that he ultimately agreed to take my $10.000.00 offer to his boss for approval. Someone I never met or even talked to before that day was that negatively triggered by the mere suggestion of shame that he came down off his high horse of "Our company doesn't entertain short sales" to being willing to take this offer to his boss.

Now before you tell me that wasn't nice, I would have to put about $25.000.00 into this property to make it salable so my number wasn't that far off. My philosophy in Real Estate investment was that it is only an offer. If you accept my offer, you may not be mad at me. If you have a better offer, please take that one instead of mine.

This is the power of shame, even with a perfect stranger. We all cringe and curl up when we think of shame. All emotions are tied to previous experiences. Shame triggers so many emotions in all of us. It is said that nothing is more demeaning and hurtful to a child than having someone they care about invoking shame on them. Please, please don't ever use it on someone you Love. I will now climb down off my own high horse and get back on track.

Lest I leave you hanging on the short sale story, before we could put it all together, I took my dream job which required me to divest myself of my Real Estate Investment business. I was sad that I couldn't help that nice couple out from under what was obviously a predatory lender. I did turn it over to a fellow investor with the stipulation that he require this nice couple be held harmless. I think he finally bought it and rehabbed it.

As Grandparents we can find other approaches while we are with our Grandkids. I vote for Good Seeing and Good Saying.

Now let's get granular about these platforms and their best use for us and our Grandchildren.

Part A. Useful platforms for Grandparents to observe and possibly be engaged on.

Most of you that are reading this book are active on Facebook for your own entertainment, to find and stay connected to family, old friends and some group support or another. There is a lot for Grandparents on this platform. I find the support groups particularly useful. There are all kinds of these to be found. I am not sure of this but most of the good ones are the ones you must join and agree to certain guidelines such as being civil, kind and supportive. Some groups are actually moderated.

All of the groups in the AARP community are moderated and the quality of conversation and the support is greatly improved because of it. I could easily name all the ones I have been a part of in the past and the ones I still do participate in, but they may not help you find your best-for-you groups. Just type in a word in search and you will find a ton of them.

As I stated in the general area most young people pre-teen and up are migrating away from Facebook. The younger Grandkids are usually a part of Mom or Dad's pages. I find these pages to be a great place to scavenge family photos of my Grands and stay up to date on what is going on with the Grandkids in that family. My favorite thing is that it reminds me of everybody's birthday. This is also a great place to find tidbits to include in your affirming Tweets to your Grandkids. And for those of us who forget a lot, this is probably the best platform at serving up that information on a silver platter.

I have found a lot of old friends on Facebook as well, and a few have found me. I feel I must qualify the videos that are automatically served up to you.

There are some good ones, but it is like trying to find the actual grass clumps in my front yard of dandelions, crabgrass, and weeds. You must filter out a lot of them to find the good ones. Having said that, if you use it in an appropriate way, I find it to be useful for most Grandparents.

I have noticed an uptick in unscrupulous people pirating sites and an unusual amount of people putting up phishing sites. These are sites with friend requests of people you already are friends with, but they have been pirated. These usually only have one or two pictures on them and not many friends, usually none of them are mutual friends. Learn about the do's and don'ts. Just ask the young folks and use your best judgment and you will be fine.

Now to the mother lode of what your Grandkids do when their heads are bent in the permanent downward position. Here are the top 4 platforms that most young folks are using regularly. It will serve us well to understand that the payoff for these various platforms is engagement. I will deal later in this chapter with online safety in general. Please be aware that the currency for these platforms is gaining a following. This alone tends to breed and encourage some risky behavior by some of the contributors. This is all the more reason you should be aware of these and other places on the internet where your Grandkids spend time and attention. My hope is to give you a look behind the curtain of the online information that is available to all. You can browse these platforms without having to sign up. I highly recommend you check them out and then talk with your Grandkids about which ones they are on and what they think of them. Have no fear, if you are just browsing these, they won't bite.

The media they offer for you to check the platforms out is relatively innocuous. I am sure there is some nefarious stuff going on, but I don't care to do that much research for this book. I do promise that you will be enlightened, and this exercise can be a great way to connect with your Grandkids. Who knows, you may even want to get an account and if your

Grandchild is in agreement, you may use these platforms to communicate with them. This is the mode of communication for most young people now. Some Grandparents join the parents by signing up just to observe and keep an eye on what is going on with their Grandchildren's own channels and engagements.

I find that most young people are on TikTok, primarily to share short videos with their friends. Things like views they like, places they are going, and stuff like dances are popular. You can go to TikTok and check it out yourself. You don't have to sign up to check it out. Just type TikTok into your browser and you will see one option to Watch now. Click that and check it out. They are videos from 3 seconds to 10 minutes and those that have a TikTok account can follow the creator of the video if they like it. Not to get in the weeds with details, it is like all Social Media platforms, it can be benign or crazy. I suggest you check it out. You will come away with two insights. First and foremost, it offers you a peek into the world of young people and their media, and second, some of them are hilarious. Happy surfing.

The second and third most popular are pretty well equal, and most kids are on both. They are Instagram and Snapchat.

Instagram is a video platform that has a comment section, much like Facebook. Once again it offers you a view inside of what many young people are consuming online these days. You can check it out without having to sign in. Just type Instagram into your browser and click on the first entry on the left side of the screen. When it comes up click Explore and you can peer behind the curtain of your Grandchildren's world. Don't worry, you can't do anything wrong, you can only learn. One of the things they like about this platform is that they can play around with silly filters and come up with some of the wackiest things imaginable. They use this to exchange text, photos, etc. Enjoy your trip into their world online.

Snapchat is a lot like Instagram. Most young folks are on both. I am not sure of the nuances but once again it is a great place to see what is going on for them. When you type Snapchat in your browser to just check it out without having to sign up you will see an option, about 5 blue highlighted headers down that says The Fastest Way to Share, click that and you can scroll down and see the content.

Most everyone, including our Grandkids, are on Twitter (Now called X). Twitter interacts with some of these other platforms. There is a difference between X and Texting. Texting is primarily a mobile phone network function that has a length limit. Depending on your phone plan there is a charge for texting.

X on the other hand is more of a social networking platform much like Instagram and Snapchat but with a limit of 289 characters. Text requires a mobile phone while X does not.

It goes beyond the scope of this chapter to explain all the intricacies of the use and interactions of these platforms. Truthfully it goes beyond this writer's ability to even comprehend those intricacies and interactions. Some of this mystery is baked into the platforms and their algorithms and the rest are left up to the creativity and knowledge only possessed by our Grandkids themselves. A lot depends on just how involved and engaged they are. As you will glean from the next section of this book, it is wise and useful to include your Grandkids in this part of the conversation.

Part B. Brave Grandparents who are on these platforms.

The research for this section was a real eye opener for me. The numbers of Grandparents that are already on these platforms are in the millions. Here is a glimpse at some of what goes on in this Social Media world.

On TikTok I ran across an 87-year-old Grandpa with 2 million followers. It seems he and his granddaughter create wholesome content that has to do with the current trends. I bow in admiration to them both.

This also occurs on Snapchat and Instagram. Grandparents are connecting with their Grandkids by staying informed about these technologies that their Grandkids are using every day. There exists a plethora of Grandparents being silly with their Grandkids. Some are willing to put themselves out there and participate in a dance or skit with the younger folks. This allows grandparents to show interest in their grandchildren's activities and stay connected in the digital age.

Additionally, a guide to online safety for grandparents has been created to help them keep kids safe while using online platforms. These examples illustrate how grandparents are leveraging Social Media platforms to bridge the generational gap and stay connected with their grandchildren.
As I have openly admitted I am new to this space alongside my Grandkids, but I am determined to learn and be there with them. The theme here should be connection and observation.

Participation with them adds an additional set of eyes and ears to what their world is like. This can only offer good results and who knows, it may be fun.

I will remind you that early on in this book I advocated for you to be you. It is perfectly understandable for you to take a pass on the Social Media train. I just want you to be aware and keep that door open. It is not going anywhere.

Part C. Online Safety

I'm not a fan of lists but there are sufficient threats that are unique to the internet and some to these Social Networking Platforms.

Here goes; Scams, Phishing, Predators, Fakes, Cyberbullying, and the two that I worry most about when it comes to my precious Grandchildren, the insidious harm to their self-esteem and the fact that these platforms are designed to create a near addiction that keeps the kids engaged. These are all the more reasons for each of us who care for the well-being of these young and impressionable minds, to learn what is necessary to combat the negative draws of Social Media.

If you are like me, you may have fallen victim to some of this already.

The good news is that there are answers to each of these and there are things like parental controls, learning about how these things are perpetuated and constantly monitoring coupled with discussions with our Grandkids and their parents. This can be a minefield if left to take its own course.

Each platform has information about the parental controls on that platform. It is good that in addition to the parents we also become familiar with these controls so we can reinforce what the parents are doing in this area.

As you have noticed, I am the eternal optimist, so I see an upside to all of this guard-railing stuff. I find this an opportunity for me to go, hat in hand, as I often do and ask my Grandchild for some help. If you listen well as they explain these different platforms to you it will reveal a lot of what is important to each of them at that stage in their lives. If you ask, for instance, why that is important to them and/or their friends and listen intently, there are clues in those answers. So, yes, I see this as just one more chance for Lasting Meaningful Connection with your Grandchildren by meeting them where they are. Kind of like a Twofer. That is my version of a Win-Win.

This approach saves you from "The Lecture" that kids resist anyway, and you learn more about them.

The most dangerous and insidious of the potential dangers on social networks is Cyberbullying. Cyberbullying refers to the use of digital technologies, such as the internet and Social Media, to harass, intimidate, or harm others. This form of bullying can take various forms, including sending hurtful messages, spreading rumors, sharing embarrassing information or images, and engaging in online social exclusion. Cyberbullying can occur through various online platforms, including Social Media sites, messaging apps, online forums, and gaming platforms.

The impact of cyberbullying on young people can be significant and wide-ranging. Here are some ways in which it can affect them:

Emotional and Psychological Effects:
- Stress and Anxiety: Victims may experience heightened stress and anxiety due to the fear of ongoing harassment and the potential for public humiliation.
- Depression: Persistent cyberbullying can contribute to feelings of sadness and hopelessness, leading to depression in some cases.

Social Consequences:
- Isolation: Victims may withdraw from social activities both online and offline, leading to isolation.
- Damage to Relationships: Cyberbullying can strain relationships with peers and friends, as well as damage the victim's reputation.

Academic Impact:
- Decline in Academic Performance: The emotional toll of cyberbullying can negatively affect concentration and academic performance.
- School Avoidance: Some victims may avoid school to escape the harassment, impacting their education.

Physical Health Consequences:
- Sleep Disturbances: Stress and anxiety from cyberbullying can lead to sleep disturbances and related health issues.
- Eating Disorders: In severe cases, cyberbullying may contribute to the development of eating disorders or other physical health problems.

Long-Term Consequences:
- Self-Esteem Issues: Cyberbullying can erode self-esteem, making it challenging for victims to develop a positive self-image.
- Potential for Self-Harm: In extreme cases, the emotional distress caused by cyberbullying may contribute to self-harm or suicidal thoughts.

Cybersecurity Concerns:
- Online Safety: Victims may become more cautious about their online activities, impacting their ability to freely engage in the digital world.

It's essential for parents, educators, and communities to be aware of cyberbullying, take preventive measures, and provide support to those affected. Promoting digital literacy, teaching empathy, and fostering open communication can help create a safer online environment for young people. Additionally, reporting mechanisms and anti-bullying policies on online platforms can contribute to addressing and preventing cyberbullying incidents.

Some of the other potholes on this road to Social Maturity are things like Sexting or putting too much personal information online. The Digital footprint is not like the one you leave in the sand at the beach. Anything you put online is there to stay. There are no take backs. This is why it is so important to ask the parents how you can help them to protect your Grandkids on these Social Media sites.

After all this Monster in the closet talk, I think it valuable to recognize that our kids aren't stupid. They derive some pretty significant fun, entertainment, and connections with their friends on these platforms. They wouldn't work so well if there wasn't a payoff for our kids. Again, I think it was Tyler Perry's Grandma who told him "If the mountain was flat the view from its top wouldn't be very spectacular." Like life, there is good and not so good stuff on these sites. They are very much a part of our kid's reality and consequently, our reality. No one sees them going away anytime soon, so we have another challenge on this Journey.

This section is so long because it is so important, and I happen to think it is one area that Grandparents can do a lot to affect better outcomes for all involved. Just because something is complicated doesn't give us a pass. Our Grandkids are and will be on these platforms so now what do we do?

Enough said about Social Media, now how about media in general? I offer two possible guardrails. First is to watch things like the news with your Grandkids and discuss it when possible. This is that light of day deal again. The other is a great resource when it comes to media. It is called "Family media tool." This is the result of the research efforts of the American Academy of Pediatrics. This is a trusted and well-established organization that can be found at www.healthychildren.org.

Chapter 13

SOME OF THE RESOURCES

> "When every physical and mental resource is focused,
> one's power to solve a problem multiplies tremendously."
>
> Norman Vincent Peale

This Journey is a lot like Parenting in many ways. We became parents and immediately started searching for the owner's manual. I don't know about you all but neither of my two extraordinary children came with one. It was at this point that I did the next best thing. I sought out others who had gone down the same road and incorporated "SOME" of their ideas for my two cherubim. Note the word SOME. Just like in your family our circumstances match exactly zero others I searched out. It was up to us as parents to do the absolute best we could by our two kids. I am happy to report that some 50 plus years later, both of them still call and check up on Ole Dad. I must be honest, this has more to do with Grace and a willingness to learn from others than with my intellect or skills as a parent.

I am an advocate of gathering information from credible sources and filtering that info, and then tailoring it to my circumstances. The good news is that with the advent of Baby Boomers becoming Grandparents there is an ever-increasing number of ideas and experiences being shared freely and abundantly. There is a lot of good information available. One very interesting source is an organization called Grandparents Academy. A young man by the name of Aaron

Larson brought forward the wonderful experiences he had with his Grandparents and assembled a team of experts in various disciplines specific to Grandparenting in a very effective way. He can be reached by going to GrandparentingAcademy.com.

Because of Aaron's foresight, expertise, and effort, this is growing into the go-to site to learn the latest and greatest accurate and timely information for Grandparents. I have watched as Aaron has created a place to gather some of the best authorities on Grandparenting and organized them into an easy to use and helpful format for those of us who want to do all we can for our Grandchildren. Experts like many times published authors in the field of Parenting and now Grandparenting, Richard and Linda Eyre. Linda and Richard have created a Master Class called Grandparenting 101: What to know from the start. In addition, Arron has introduced me to an expert in Long Distance Grandparenting, Dr. Kerry Byrne, who is the Founder of "The Long-Distance Grandparent." She is by far the most effective source of information in this area of connection. You can find her at https://TheLongDistanceGrandparent.com. These sites represent just the tip of the iceberg when it comes to information. You may also want to check out GrandparentsAcademy.com

I call them various disciplines because when it comes to Grandparenting, there are many aspects and circumstances that must be considered, many opportunities to step up your game for the benefit of your Grandchildren and the entire family. If you are blessed with a stable extended family, you are among the fortunate few. For you, gratitude is appropriate. For many millions of other Grandparents, the experience is quite different.

Just this morning I had breakfast with a friend who was on his way to Jacksonville, Florida to visit his twin girls and their families. Between them he has a Grandson/Granddaughter set of twins and another Granddaughter, they are preteen and early teens. He is amongst the blessed, and he knows it.

His challenges came when he became a single parent to twin 4-year-old daughters while still being a member of the Armed Forces. He made it work until he got help from the rest of his family, and here 30+ years later he is off to visit those two wonderful daughters and three equally wonderful Grandkids. As it turns out he had an extraordinary visit with his 13-year-old Granddaughter who is Autistic. This was his first opportunity to really be able to bond with her. He has learned how to enter her world, and the benefits were some fun and meaningful conversations during their walks together. His comment to me was that he discovered more about her world on this trip than any before. I was affirmed in my own belief that the outcome is better when you meet them where they are. She is lucky to have such a Grandfather.

Most of us have at least a few challenges, to varying degrees, when it comes to our extended families. You will find that most of the credible people who write about extended family will have information about how to handle the various fallout due to the more challenging branches of those families. These cover a broad spectrum, from an ex-in-law or two, to multiple layers of family dysfunction.

I spent years writing about the extremes of extended family dysfunction and complete alienation. It is a sad situation and I had to move toward the light of hope and write about the majority of reasonably functional families. Fortunately, the norm is that a large percentage of your extended family will likely have found a way to get along. This doesn't absolve you of the work required to follow the best path in order to keep it that way. In the latter chapters of this book, I will offer some best practices and many resources that are specific to some of these extended family issues. For those that are intentional Grandparents there will be mostly good outcomes but there will be some that may require you to reach deep down inside yourself as well as finding outside help and affirmation during troubled times.

I also find some great information in the digital issues of Grand Magazine. This can be found at Grandmagazine.com. Just as a teaser, the particular issue I am reading features Sir Richard Branson. He is a British business magnate and commercial astronaut. He also founded the Virgin Group, which today controls more than 400 companies in various fields. In Grand Magazine he is referred to as "The Grand Dude." This same issue celebrates the 20th Anniversary of The Ga Ga Sisterhood (Love that name) which is a refreshing social network for enthusiastic, creative women who join together to indulge in the joy of being Grandmothers. Just know that all of the pertinent subjects are covered well in this magazine. It is one of my go-to sources.

Over the past decades the resources for Grandparents have exploded. Not only are there many good sources of stories that help us know that we are not alone on our journey, there are also a plethora of programs and organizations that have formed and matured to the point that they are functioning wonderfully to offer hands-on help. Some of these groups are governmental like your local Council on Aging, as well as many other concerned folks helping make this planet a much better place, especially for our Grandchildren.

One good example is our local Cape Fear YWCA which sponsors a chapter of the Grandparent Support Network. They specifically support Grandparents caring for their Grandchildren (Our Grand Heroes). A great and noble endeavor. The predominant website in the area of Grandparents Raising their Grandchildren is an offshoot of Generations United (GU.org). This site is called GrandFamilies.org. It is sites like these that will lead you to any possible help that you may need if you find yourself a part of the 1.6 million Grandparents who are raising their Grandchildren.

There are more and more books, some narrowly niched and others like this one that offer considered and valuable information and ideas about your Journey.

The spin-off of this book is a companion website aptly titled, GoodToGreatGrandparenting.com. This is intended to be an ever-evolving more in-depth source for ideas, success stories, networking opportunities, and anything that will make more Good Grandparents Great. One source for Grandparents dealing with things like limited or non-existent visitations is CaringGrandparents.com which also has a Facebook page by the same name.

The other trusted source is one I have used for years with my own Grandparenting quest, and also for research in my writing about Grandparenting, AARP.Org. This is a repository of lots of valuable information that is targeted to our demographic. Their resources are sufficient and their help for Grandparents is massive. They have moderated groups and blogs dedicated just to Grandparenting. They present some well-written articles from some credible journalists. They have probably done the best job of providing the most diverse and informative narrative about all things Grandparenting over the years, and I have enjoyed being part of the discussion group communities for some time now. These are moderated groups, so they tend to stay more on point than some of the Facebook groups do.

When it comes to hands-on resources the table is better set today with some amazing organizations and programs to help Grandparents. This is especially true when it comes to situations like Grandparents raising Grandchildren, Families in crisis, Legal entanglement, etc.

These resources range from financial help, food assistance, advocacy, respite care, support groups, etc. In addition to some government organizations, Church and Community groups are flourishing. These groups and programs that provide support, resources, and assistance to families in these challenging situations, can be found through your grandchild's school, area agencies on aging, communities and senior centers, faith-based organizations and child services agencies.

It is important to consider all the changes going on in the Grandparenting space. Please note that I said consider. As a discerning Good Grandparent working on Great, only you can judge what is best for your family and Grandkids. Not all information is a miracle fix for what is going on in some families. If you will remember I said in the Introduction to this book, "trust your own ability to create a Great outcome." This is a lot to take in and digest. You are to be applauded for being a Caring Grandparent as well as your willingness to take this Journey.

Chapter 14

ABOUT THE HOW + More Resources

> "The illiterate of the future will not be the person who cannot read. It will be the person who does not know how to learn."
>
> Alvin Toffler

Those of you who are still reading this are MY people. You are on the path, and for that I commend you. Your Grandchildren are doubly blessed by your "Entering the Arena." As I have tried to make clear throughout this book, the majority of us are just trying to be the best we know how to be at this Grandparenting role. If your eyes have been opened to more possibilities and opportunities to adjust your path, then my mission is fulfilled.

As I stated early-on in the book, the term easy isn't always part of the Journey. Having run through many possible horrific scenarios that can come from these extended and/or blended families which seem to be more prevalent these days, I want to wrap this up with a few thoughts. Thoughts about how much easier it is to go forth knowing that we have given this Journey a really good effort, and that having done so, our Grandchildren are more empowered, more secure in who they are and feeling more Loved. The magic is that we are so much better Grandparents for taking this Journey. If your effort was great your outcome stands a good chance of being great as well. The beauty of being a Good to Great Grandparent is that it is your individual Journey, and it is perfectly fine for you to undertake it at your own pace and in your own way.

After being flooded with ideas, potential roadblocks, inspiration, and information, you have a better idea of how you fit into this role that you have been gifted. My hope is that you have learned more about this immense and important subject of Grandparenting in the 21st century.

Your challenge is to individualize your path. Find the one that offers both you and your Grandchildren the greatest outcome.

Here, in a nutshell are what Some of the Most Successful Grandparenting models look like. Please reread that sentence, I said SOME and MOST successful, Not All and Perfectly Successful. I am not sure the latter exists so give yourself and your family a break.

PLANTING THE SEEDS OF "FOOD FOR THOUGHTFULNESS".

Assess and plan. Your family is like no other. Especially your extended family. While it is important for you to assess each significant member of your entire family, it is more important to evaluate how you wish to fit into each situation given the circumstances of the situation. Arm yourself with as much knowledge as possible and decide how you want to interact in a given situation. Your greatest asset will be your thoughtfulness of who you are and what you wish to accomplish in your role as a Grandparent or a Great-Grandparent.

If you have 3 hours to do an assessment of what kind of Grandparent you wish to be, you will do well to spend 2 ½ of those hours on who you are, what you like, what you are good at, and what you most value. By figuring out what you want this Journey to look like, instead of how your skills, etc. fit into this extended family, you will find yourself on a path to better contribution to your Grandchildren and greater self-fulfillment.

Proceed with thoughtfulness. Becoming a New Grandparent for the very first time or like me becoming a Great-Great Grandparent for the very first time is still a miracle. As a miracle it deserves to be revered as such.

Each time a new miracle occurs in your family a new family unit is created. No matter how you have acted or reacted in the past, this is a new opportunity to apply the wisdom of the 21st century Grandparent. Please remember that your intention up until now is not being questioned. The world has moved forward, and your best outcomes will occur if you recognize that and practice at least these three principles of Grandparenting a new Grandchild. I am in no way asking you to agree with these principles, I am merely sharing the top three best practices in today's world of Grandparenting.

1. Respect boundaries and rules: Be supportive and respectful of the new parents' decisions and preferences. Avoid offering unsolicited advice and be mindful of their boundaries. Remember that it's not a competition with other grandparents, and your role is to be the best grandparent you can be, not to interfere in their relationship with the baby.

2. Offer help and support: Be proactive in offering assistance to the new parents. Ask what they need and how you can get involved to make their lives easier. Make specific offers. Help with tasks like running errands, making meals, or cleaning up. Offer to take care of the baby while the parents rest or attend to other responsibilities.

3. Follow the parents' lead: Stick to the rules and guidelines set by the new parents, even if you disagree or think you know better. Allow them the opportunity to learn and develop as parents, and to make mistakes if necessary. Remember that your role is to support and encourage them, not to take over or undermine their authority.

Staying connected to your Grandchild.

Depending on so many variables of your extended family, this may seem like an easy task. You Love your Grandchildren and they know it. This may be an easy task in a fantasy world but in the 21st century, not so much. There are forces within and outside of your control. I suggest that you will do well to consider the direction given in Luke 12:34 and 35 in the New American Bible (Revised Edition); **34** For where your treasure is, there also will be your heart, be Vigilant and Faithful Servants.[a] **35** "Gird your loins and light your lamps.

If you refuse to recognize these principles, you do it at your own peril. These are real forces in the real world of today. I don't like some of them either, but please consider them for the sake of your precious Grandkids.

Honor the parents' wishes: If you were a perfect parent, you may be exempt from this principle. The rest of us are bound by this singularly important rule of the road. The more thoughtful you are of the parents, the better your odds of a Lasting Meaningful Connections to your Grandchild.

Get involved in their interests.
- Practice active listening.
- Listen to learn, not necessarily to respond.
- Spend quality time together.
- Utilize technology when possible.
- Create your own family traditions.

What can get in the way?
- Unresolved conflict and trauma.
- A manipulative Grandparent or Parent.
- Ill-considered angry words or statements.

- Parents' misuse of their control of contact.
- Emotional manipulation.
- Financial manipulation.
- Secret keeping.
- Threatening correspondence.

These and other behaviors are a harbinger of things to come. As you can imagine, some of these behaviors are really hard to defend. The only hope for defense starts with awareness.

Remember your most important resources are genuine love, intention, attention, and respect. Be present, patient, and flexible as you adapt to these changing behaviors, needs and personalities. Building strong connections takes time and effort, but the rewards are invaluable.

The best resources for staying connected to your grandchildren will depend on a few factors, like their age, your proximity, and preferred modes of communication. But no matter what, creating lasting meaningful connections is all about nurturing the unique bond you share.

Here are some ideas to get you started.

Traditional communication:

- Phone calls: Schedule regular phone calls to simply chat and hear about their day.
- Snail mail: Handwritten letters, postcards, or care packages add a personal touch that text messages can't replicate. Share stories, jokes, or small treasures. Remember to use their favorite colors, themes, superheroes, etc. Personalized snail mail is much more effective and long remembered. Things like envelopes of their favorite color, Stickers or drawings on the outside of the envelope, etc. People Love lumpy mail.

- Audiobooks to be discussed: Or choose a book you both enjoy and take turns reading chapters aloud, each recording yours and sending it to the other. It's like a virtual audible book club!

Technology:

- Video calls: Apps like Zoom, Skype, and FaceTime are fantastic for virtual visits. Share meals, read stories, play games, or just catch up face-to-face.
- Social Media: Follow their pages on platforms they use (with their permission), send them fun messages, and engage with their posts. This shows you're interested in their world. This is also a great way to look into their world and also to notice if there are any red flags that come up.
- Digital photo frames: Send them pictures from your daily life and vice versa. It's a constant reminder of how much you care.
- Online games: Play word games, trivia, or even collaborative creations like digital stories together.

Shared activities:

- Start a book club: Choose a series or genre you both like and discuss each book via video calls or phone.
- Learn a new skill together: Whether it's baking, coding, gardening, or playing an instrument, learning something new is a fun way to bond and create shared memories.
- Virtual experiences: Explore museums, zoos, or aquariums online together. You can even have pretend "field trips" and discuss what you saw.
- Creative projects: Work on collaborative art projects, choose a charitable project to collaborate on, write stories together, or even compose a song! The possibilities are endless.

Just a few additional resources:

- Websites: Grandparents.com, Read Brightly (Readbrightly.com), and The Glen Retirement System (theglen.org) offer articles, tips, and activity ideas for connecting with grandchildren. Grandparents.com, The National Grandparents Program, Zero to Three's Grand Connector program
- Books: "Brightly Storytime: Nana the Great Goes Camping" and "How to Connect with Your Grandchildren" by Psyche Guides are filled with heartwarming stories and practical advice. "The Whole-Brain Child" by Daniel J. Siegel and Tina Payne Bryson, "Grandparenting in the 21st Century" by Carol Banko Ronning
- Podcasts: The Go-To Grandma, Adventures with Grammy, The Cool-Grandpa
- Local programs: Check your community centers, libraries, or senior centers for workshops or events for grandparents and grandchildren.

Keep in mind, the most important thing is to be present, engaged, and show your grandchildren how much you love them. Choose activities and communication methods that fit your style and theirs, and most importantly, have fun together!

Chapter 15

YOUR NEXT CHAPTER

> " Successful people maintain a positive focus in life no matter what is going on around them. They stay focused on their past successes rather than their past failures, and on the next action steps they need to take to get them closer to the fulfillment of their goals rather than all the other distractions that life presents to them."
>
> Jack Canfield

If you recall in the chapter where we were discussing things that don't work as well as we had hoped, I mentioned "It is what you do next that counts". No matter what has transpired before now or where you find yourself on your Journey "It is what you do next that counts".

It is often the small things that make the greatest difference. I urge you to do some action different than you were doing when you started this book. A tweet, a note, a call. At the least take a look at some of the resources for more ideas, try social media, join a Grandparenting group, visit Grandparenting websites to learn more. This journey is not an osmosis process. Your results will be commensurate with your imagination and efforts. The magic lies in the reciprocal value you will gain by each and every action you take. Ain't life Grand?

Neil Taft

I have done my level best to share what I have learned about Grandparenting with you, now you can improve on what you have read and that will get me closer to my goal of creating more Love and Connection in the lives of these precious souls we get to call Grandchildren and at the same time help Grandparents to become the best they can be. You are now a lot closer to your Highest and Best Grandparenting self. Congratulations you are well on your way to enjoying Lasting Meaningful Connections with your Grandchildren. Thank You for being a Caring Grandparent. Have a Great Journey.

www.ingramcontent.com/pod-product-compliance
Lightning Source LLC
Chambersburg PA
CBHW082105140626
46553CB00018B/736